Fire in the ⅼ
The Alchemy of

Edited and Introduced by Stanton Marlan

Chiron Publications

Wilmette, Illinois

Library of Congress Catalog Card Number: 97-31742

Printed at Coach House Printing, Toronto, Canada
Copyedited by Roger E. Riendeau
Cover design by D. J. Hyde

Library of Congress Cataloguing-in-Publication Data:

Fire in the stone: the alchemy of desire / edited and introduced by
    Stanton Marlan.
        p.   cm.
    Includes bibliographical references.
    ISBN 1-888602-06-6 (hardcover) ISBN 1-888602-05-8 (paperback)
    1. Jungian psychology. 2. Psychoanalysis. I. Marlan, Stanton.
BF173.F498 1997
150.19′54—dc21   97-31742
                                                      CIP

A thousand praises!
A thousand hearts of gratitude!
For your love has given wings to the world

Jelaluddin Rumi (1207-73)

I dedicate this book

To the memory of my grandparents, Sam and Ida Markowitz

To my father, Jack Marlan, and the memory of my mother, Sylvia Marlan

To my brother, David, and my uncle Milton

To my wife, Jan, and my children, Dawn, Tori, and Brandon, and my grandson, Malachi Marlan-Librett

... All intimately involved in the alchemy of my soul-making

List of Figures

Contents

Contributors

Stanton Marlan, PhD, ABPP, is a Jungian analyst and clinical psychologist. He is the Director of the C.G. Jung Institute Analyst Training Program of Pittsburgh and a coordinator and training analyst for the Inter-Regional Society of Jungian Analysts. He holds diplomates in both clinical psychology and psychoanalysis from the American Board of Professional Psychology, and he is a member of the New York, Inter-Regional, and International Jungian Societies. He is the editor of *Salt and the Alchemical Soul* (Spring Publications, 1995).

James Hillman, PhD, is the former Director of Studies at the C.G. Jung Institute at Zurich. He is the father of archetypal psychology and a world-renowned author of many works including *The Myth of Analysis* (1972), *Revisioning Psychology* (1975), and *The Soul's Code* (1997).

Paul K. Kugler, PhD, is President of the Inter-Regional Society of Jungian Analysts. He is the author of numerous works ranging from contemporary psychoanalysis to experimental theatre and postmodernism. His most recent publications are: *Supervision: Jungian Perspectives on Clinical Supervision* (1995) and "Psychic Imaging: A Bridge between Object and Subject" in *The Cambridge Companion to Jung,* edited by Polly Young-Eisendrath and Terrence Dawson (1997).

Patricia Berry, PhD, is a graduate of the University of Dallas and the C.G. Jung Institute, Zurich. She is past President of the Inter-Regional Society of Jungian Analysts and current President of the New England Society of Jungian Analysts. She is in private practice in Cambridge, Massachusetts. Her writings include: *Echo's Subtle Body: Contributions to an Archetypal Psychology* (Spring Publications, 1992).

Donald E. Kalsched, PhD, is a Clinical Psychologist and Jungian Analyst in private practice in Katonah, New York. He is a faculty member and supervisor at the C.G. Jung Institute in New York

City. He is also Dean of Jungian Studies at the Westchester Institute for Training in Psychoanalysis and Psychotherapy in Mt. Kisco, New York.

Lionel Corbett, MD, trained in medicine and Psychiatry in England and as a Jungian Analyst at the C.G. Jung Institute of Chicago. He is currently on the faculty of Pacifica Graduate Institute in Santa Barbara, California and has recently published *The Religious Function of the Psyche* (Routledge, 1996).

Ronald Schenk, PhD, is a Jungian Analyst, teaching and practicing in Dallas and Houston, Texas where he also serves as a senior training analyst for the Inter-Regional Society of Jungian Analysts. His book *The Soul of Beauty: A Psychological Investigation of Appearance* (1992) gives an aesthetic foundation to depth psychology. Current writing interests focus on cultural depth psychology, Jung and post-modern concerns, and clinical training.

Scott Churchill, PhD, is Chair of the Department of Psychology at the University of Dallas where he has taught since 1981. Currently, he is writing a methodological text in phenomenological psychology and is engaged in a joint research project with the Dallas Zoological Society to study the social behaviors of a group of captive chimpanzees. He has also served as Editor of *Methods: A Journal for Human Science* since 1990 and associate Editor of the *Journal of Theoretical and Philosophical Psychology* since 1986.

Acknowledgements

I would like to thank the Inter-Regional Society of Jungian Analysts for the opportunity to host and moderate our fall conference on Alchemy and Seduction here in Pittsburgh, and for their support for the inclusion of some of the proceedings in this book. Particular thanks is due to Paul Kugler who support the process from the beginning, and to my colleagues whose excellent papers are included in this book.

My thanks go out to Murray Stein and Nathan Schwartz-Salant for their critical insight and interest in publishing these essays. Thanks also to Roger Riendeau whose editorial production expertise helped significantly to shape the text.

I also wish to extend my appreciation to the members of the C.G. Jung Institute Analyst Training Program of Pittsburgh and the C.G. Jung Educational Center of Pittsburgh for support of my teaching and research. Thanks to John Pavlic, Director of the Fisher Collection of Alchemical Pictures at the Fisher Scientific Company who gave of his time to enrich the experience of the conference out of which this book emerged

Thanks to my colleague Gene Monick for the use of his personal story included in the text, and to Keith Knecht, and artists Lynne Cannoy, Janet Tobin, and Roger Gibson of the C.G. Jung Educational Center for their continuing support of the project. Thanks is also due to my friend John Shulman of Caliban Books for his ongoing research support, and to my friends Terry Pulver and Roger Brooke for their astute intellectual interest and dialogue. I further wish to express appreciation to the analytic candidates and auditors of the Pittsburgh Seminar of the Inter-Regional Society of Jungian Analysts whose serious commitment to the work of analysis helps to inspire my own work.

My sincere thanks to my Jungian colleagues — Joseph Henderson, Andrew Samuels, John Beebe, Robert Bosnak, and June Singer — for their support and enthusiasm and for taking time out of their busy schedules to read and comment on the manuscript. Thanks is also due to James Hillman for his early reading and comments on my chapter and for his continuing support of my work.

Finally, I would like also to extend my special thanks and appreciation to my wife and Jungian colleague, Jan, whose careful reading and editing of my paper not only helped to make it a better paper but, as always, forwarded my own thinking.

Stanton Marlan
August 1997

Preface

The inspiration for this book emerged out of the fall conference of the Inter-Regional Society of Jungian Analysts. The conference theme was "Alchemy and Seduction," and the presentations catalyzed considerable excitement and discussion. The idea of publishing the proceedings was, in part, due to the enthusiasm of the participants and to the many requests for the papers. The following presenters committed their papers for publication: Patricia Berry, Donald Kalsched, Lionel Corbett, and Ronald Schenk.

The enthusiasm for the conference was also a result of a number of very thoughtful respondents: Joseph Wakefield, David Rosen, Judith Savage, David Sedgwick, Rosales Wynne-Roberts, and Diane Myers. The dynamics of the conference and the ideas generated by it were wide ranging, and as the idea for the book emerged, additional essays by Stanton Marlan, Paul Kugler, James Hillman, and Scott Churchill were added to the proceedings.

In all, the essays compiled in this book represent and extend what many participants found to be a vital reflection on Jungian analysis in today's world.

Introduction

Stanton Marlan

For the most part, this book is inspired by the continuing vitality of the alchemical metaphor. The idea of an "alchemy of desire" is put forth as an imagistic way of speaking about a field of relations and processes fundamental to Jung's view of the dynamic psyche. It is within this alchemical field that a reader might imagine the unfolding of the following investigations. While alchemy as an explicit theme is not central to all of the following, a majority of the essays presented here are deeply influenced by it and, for some, it is focal.

An image of the Red Stone as a goal of alchemy is taken up in the initial essay, "Fire in the Stone." Here, psyche's intentionality becomes a complex question, and as one discovers more than one relatively autonomous center of desire, our understanding of subjectivity becomes complex. Jung's use of alchemy to help understand this complexity was an attempt to find the essential aspects of the individuation process. Reading Jung as an essentialist, however, has brought his approach into critical question. While not agreeing that Jung is best read as an essentialist, the above essay follows the thought of archetypalist psychologist Hillman and post-structuralist philosophers Derrida and Heidegger because of their particular sensitivity to the shadow of essentialism and their prominence in contemporary debate. The archetypalist and deconstructionist positions are seen here to have important contributions to make to a contemporary reading of Jung and show similarities in their emphasis on particulars and in rethinking philosophical and metapsychological foundations.

In James Hillman's essay, we move from red to the "Seduction of Black," in which he explores the alchemical *nigredo* — and the fundamental darkness beyond Mecurius duplex. In his alchemical psychology, blackness is seen as a challenge to our attachment to color consciousness, our belief in a Cartesian vision of science, and our sense of clinical authority and identity. Fundamentally, blackness becomes an archetypal force necessary to correct our "bright-sightedness," our favoring of light, and our adaptation to the phenomenal world through the organ of sight. As a contrast to light, blackness has received a negative definition, and it may be that when the archetypal / structural reality is projected on to people and moralized, we have a possible matrix for our racist attitudes. Beyond the negative projection onto black, it also serves both to continually deconstruct and to shift our stagnant paradigms, as well as to shade our world, giving it depth and dimension. As such, black becomes a paradox — on the one hand, of the quintessential color of change — and on the other, a process not to be surpassed by another stage of development. Through Hillman's dark eye, Mercurius duplex, and the ease with which telos is understood as a developmental process, is brought into question and greater differentiation. In all, Hillman fundamentally challenges our ontological vision.

Concern with stagnant paradigms and commitment to ontological positions is taken up by Paul Kugler in his essay on "Childhood Seduction." He, too, is interested in fundamental concerns and how philosophical commitments can prejudice and shape the way we see our patients, their problems, and the hermeneutics by which we engage our clinical practice.

In this essay, Kugler focuses on the clinical phenomenon of childhood seduction that early preoccupied Freud and Jung and has returned to the center stage in professional debate. He confronts this issue as a clinical condition and as a social problem, but, further, sees it raising fundamental questions for depth psychology. In a significantly revised version of an earlier paper, he focuses on an analysis of the implicit assumptions of various psychoanalytic theories important to the therapeutic relationship, wanting to develop a greater appreciation of how the therapist's theory of neurosis plays a significant role in determining what is experienced as real and true in the encounter with the patient.

His analysis exposes the presuppositions implicit in current extreme positions on childhood sexual abuse, from literalist conviction to ideas about the false memory syndrome. He reviews Freud's and Jung's seduction theories and points out the limited and often selective distortions of the views held by Alice Miller, Jeffrey Masson, and Milton Kline.

Traditionally, Jungian theory attempts to integrate two classical hermeneutics, the causal and finalistic approaches, which are taken up in Patricia Berry's essay. She reflects on her sense that traditional Jungian theory gets seduced and seduces us not to take seriously enough the causal approach. For her, this is particularly a problem when dealing with victims of childhood seduction and abuse and is a shadow problem in Jungian analysis. Jungian work seems implicitly to make an ontological commitment to the finalistic approach. Clinically, this can show itself when asking a victim of abuse to carry the shadow too quickly. While Berry, like other Jungians, sees the limitation of the traditional view of the victim, she asks the larger cultural and perhaps archetypal question of the meaning of the emergence of this image in our time, and what it may be pointing toward; clinicians need to take such a question seriously when working with these patients.

The experience of being a victim may be a necessary psychological experience, moving the psyche into an emotional place from which the process of transformation can occur. She sees the reductive hermeneutic as an alchemical move in order to arrive at the prima materia which can help the patient to have a full opportunity for experience and embodiment. Berry's sense is that in the traumatized patient, there is a danger of passing on too quickly to a finalist point of view.

In Donald Kalsched's work, movement toward any kind of finalist goal from the traumatized patient is not only a danger, but is blocked by incapacitating anxiety in which archetypal defenses come into play, causing a malignant regression not unlike bodily diseases of the auto-immune system. These defenses suspend the personality in an attempt to protect the fragile ego. In such situations, the Jungian understanding of regression, the positive optimistic vision of the wisdom of the psyche, and finalistic interpretations overlook genuine pathology and can obscure the dark and seductive side of Mercurius.

For Kalsched, the archetypal energy behind this defensive "self-care system" is Hermes-Mercurius in his underworld form. Kalsched sees, in his analysis, an archetypal dimension of psychological defense, a deepened way of imagining what has been called "negative therapeutic reaction," "severe super ego states," "death instinct," "archetypal shadow and the dark side of God." He feels that more specificity is added to this phenomenon by considering the work of Fairbairn on the Internal Sabatoeur, which extends Jung's more generalized formulations. For Kalsched, it is only when this pattern can be identified and worked through that the defensive addiction to a "lesser" *coniunctio* can release the psyche to the more traditional Jungian work of individuation and teleology. When this happens, Mercurius turns another face, allowing the life-giving power of the psyche to release a "glue"-like substance that can hold the psyche and world together in an integrated way.

It is this "glue" that is taken up as a special focus by Lionel Corbett in his analysis of the Alchemical "Glutinum Mundi," the "Glue of the World." For Corbett, this can help us understand the deeper role of seduction and how it operates in analysis. It is this "glue" that constitutes the powerful motivation to be in relationships, and it is what is sought when entering analysis. For Corbett, it is more important than insight and making the unconscious conscious. Behind human sexual behavior and seductiveness is the need for cohesiveness. It is this need that is often behind the desire for overt sexual acting out, the need to be held together, and to be a cohesive personality. For Corbett, this "glue" is a mysterious compound, a secretion of the Self which is maximally secreted between people. It is a psychological matrix which allows the *coniunctio* to develop. Corbett feels this is described generally and archetypally in Jung's work on the transference, but it is only recently that it is possible to delineate the details of it. He feels this is facilitated by Kohut and the mechanisms of Self psychology's study of the Self-object. He differentiates this notion from the way it is used by object-relations theorists and by Fordham.

In returning to the pictures of the *Rosarium Philosophorum*, he interprets and elaborates the many possible meanings involved in the erotic transference in the context of the overall state of the Self. In this larger context, Corbett finds a higher energy, a seeking for cohesiveness and archetypal ordering principles that are transpersonal and which allow reorganization of the personality. For Corbett (following Jacoby), both analyst and analysand ultimately sit in a transpersonal field, the higher purpose of which, when properly grounded in the analyst, constitutes a kind of love that is not only earthy, but also a form of agape intended to bring compassionate help to the soul.

Like Corbett, Ronald Schenk, in his study of the Alchemical Extractio, also sees that the erotic attraction in analysis and the transference is not necessarily one of the genitals but emphasizes less a form of agape then of the analysts sensing. He states that in clinical practice, the therapist is most effective not when imposing a theoretical system, but when closely following or "sniffing" actual experience. Following Jung and Miller, he describes how seduction leads to "an intuitive bodily vigorous, earthy, pungently aromatic form of knowing through the nose." He describes a vision of therapy that also, like Corbett's and Hillman's, breaks down the Cartesian separation between analyst and analysand. He critiques the notion of projection and describes a model of "reciprocal flow of attraction and attracted," where the establishment of a logocentric base or source is not only impossible, but irrelevant.

Schenk's revisioning of psychotherapy and seduction stays close to the language of desire to bring about a different sense of eros than that which he feels permeates current puritanical preconceptions in psychotherapy. For Schenk, seduction, rather than being a shameful experience, is a paradigmatic situation for analysis, in which mutual seductions are a universal dynamic which extract our complexes and bring forth our essences. This revisioning suggests to Schenk that our idea of individuation and the nature of the Self must change. For him, the sense of Self is not seen as a goal of higher consciousness, but rather the goal is a process of revealing or evoking essences through the seductions and attractions spiraling between patient and therapist.

Schenk's view of mutual seductions as a universal dynamic spiraling between patient and therapist shares a vision with Scott Churchill's notion of a possible mutuality in male/female relations in general. Churchill, in his essay, takes up the question of male desire and the perception of it by many feminist authors that suggest it excludes the female as a subject and lacks mutuality in principle or practice. Churchill's concern is that men and women have fallen out of sync with each other and that, in fact, male desire has been objectified and stereotyped; he calls for a deeper understanding. For this purpose, Churchill calls on phenomenology and depth psychological formulations of male sexuality and Jung, in particular.

He focuses on the archetypal basis of the *coniunctio opposito-rum* and amplifies his discussion with the work of Merleau-Ponty and others to suggest how psychological and existential polarities get turned into dangerous opposition. His essay suggests a way of moving toward a sense of mutuality and receptivity in our inter-personal lives, and calls for a better sense of empathy between the sexes and a more benevolent, generous interpretation of the desires of the other.

In further explorations of these essays, it is hoped that the reader will discover Jungian analysis as a broad and vital disci-pline, undergoing clarification, critique, and continuing revision. As a psychoanalytic school, it forces dialogue with other analytic perspectives, and as a tradition, it continues an intimate exchange with psychological, religious, scientific, mythological, and other archetypal fields. In this collection of essays, Jungian analysis is shown to be both self-reflective and responsive to a wide range of contemporary psychological and cultural issues with implications for our understanding of childhood seduction, trauma, false memory syndrome, victimization, racism, human sexuality, femi-nism, and the issue of conflict and mutuality in the al-chemistry of the sexes.

In this book, the above themes have been treated with philo-sophical and clinical concern, and they present challenges to clas-sical theory and practice. One such challenge is a struggle with a notion of telos in the light of cases of significant pathology and trauma with regard to a vision of psychic intentionality.

The essays, as a whole, resonate with a wide range of theoret-ical perspectives within the Jungian community, from classical to post-modern, and in and through them, alchemy plays a signifi-cant role, continuing to confirm the idea of its sustaining value in the development of Jungian psychology. It is further hoped that these essays will make a contribution to practitioners, as well as to a significantly large audience, including philosophers, femi-nists, social critics, artists, those concerned with the legal system, and men and women in general who might look to Jungian psychology for continuing inquiry into contemporary life.

Chapter 1

Fire in the Stone: An Inquiry into the Alchemy of Soul-making

Stanton Marlan

> Soul making has as its goal a resurrection in beauty and plea-
> sure.... In a curious way, you and I crown matter, have been
> crowning matter, many times, perhaps since childhood. Recall
> the stones... (Hillman 1993, 261, 265).

Introduction

This reflection on what the soul wants begins and ends with
stones, and in an elementary sensate engagement with matter. As
a child, the discovery of stones filled me with an odd pleasure. I
loved to play in the dirt and saw the dark earth as a cosmos team-
ing with life. And there were the stones — alive and yet dead; they
were precious to me, and I reveled in their beauty and in their variety of shapes, sizes, colors, and textures.

I collected them and returned to this play daily. There was
something enigmatic — foreign — about them, yet in some way
more intimate than the world of human discourse. With the
stones I was alone, yet not alone. They held a secret, and my
secret was with them. As I grew up and this experience began to
fade, I continued to have moments of reconnection with the place
in my soul that was touched by them. I remember one night
having a vision of being an anthropologist from another world in
the future. I had landed on earth and was walking around; everything seemed new and interesting, particularly the stones scat-
tered on the ground. They had a numinous aura, as if they were
jewels lying there free for all to enjoy, an open treasure.

Over the years I have continued to take pleasure in, and
wonder about, stones. I would occasionally bring them home to
set on a shelf or desk and enjoy their natural beauty that contained
many memories from childhood and extended into a mystery that

seemed to stand on a threshold between myself and some other, between life and the beyond, between ego and the unknown. In later years, as I developed an interest in alchemy, I was naturally intrigued by the fact that one of the most pervasive images of its goal was the lapis or philosopher's stone, an image as compelling as the original stones of childhood and whose meaning remains elusive.

In his essay, "Concerning the Stone: Alchemical Images of the Goal," James Hillman asks: "Why the stone? What, in particular, does this image of the goal say to the soul?" (1993, 249). In this work, he sets out again to respond to the question: "what does the soul want?" He explicitly asked this question in his earlier work, *Healing Fiction* (1983, 83). The direction of my essay was inspired and given focus by the above works, which seem naturally linked and also bring the question of the soul's desire to yet another level of articulation. Together, they form a matrix for the following reflection on psyche's purpose.

Psyche's Purpose: What Does the Soul Want?

That psyche has a purpose and exhibits an intentionality beyond ego consciousness was one of C.G. Jung's assumptions and contributions to libido theory, as well as to a vision of a creative unconscious (Jung 1956, 137). The question, "what does the soul want?" (Hillman 1983, 185; 1993; Jung 1956, 137), is a way of posing this question of intentionality, and it is a question at the heart of a Jungian psychology. The notion of a creative process at the core of human existence is a way of imagining the question of intentionality, and it predates analytic theory in our earliest attempts to visualize life's energies. From mythology and philosophy, Jung gives examples of such numinous images, citing the cosmogonic significance of Eros in Hesiod; the Orphic figure of Phanes, the shining one and first created father of Eros; and the Indian god of love Kama, who is, as well, a cosmogonic principal. From the pre-Socratics through Plato and Aristotle, and from the Neoplatonists down through modern and contemporary philosophers, images that suggest life has a creative purpose have permeated the thoughts of mankind (Jung 1956, 137).

In all the above, life's creative desire is never simply equated with what a person consciously wants. Creative desire is beyond the ego and, at times, demands a complex play between a personal and a cosmogonic force, and this complexity is likewise found in Jung's vision. Jung demonstrated that psyche's intention was not identical with the conscious will. This problematized any simple understanding of subjectivity and lies at the core of Jungian theorizing. At the simplest level, with Freud and Jung respectively, we learn we are not masters in our own house and that the desires of the soul seem to have a mind of their own and can often master us. The architecture of Jungian thought is rooted in this paradoxical awareness, and it has led over time to an enlarged vision of psyche with the development of personified notions such as the shadow, anima, and other archetypal structures that seem to exhibit relatively autonomous aims, often departing from conscious intention. Discovering more than one autonomous center of desire reveals a field of tensions fundamental to Jung's view of psyche's dynamics.

For Jung, binary oppositions were prominent and the theme of his last major work, *Mysterium Coniunctionis*, in which the tension of opposites animates the individuation process, the aim and intention of which seems to be the constellation of a larger center of personality capable of embracing divergences of the Soul. Jung calls this larger structure the Self. It is as if this Self has a purpose that exceeds our competing desires, and/or opposes or complements varying desires which can be glimpsed only from a perspective not totally identified with the ego or any other complex. One may then begin to differentiate the desire of the ego from the desire of other figures of psyche and from what Jung ultimately felt was the larger architect of the Soul.

How Then to Know What the Soul Wants: The Turn to Classical Alchemy

For Jung, classical alchemy was an important source of information for understanding the above processes and for gaining a widened perspective on psychological transformation. Alchemy served him, in part, as a paradigmatic model of the individuation process and, as Edward Edinger (1985) has noted, as a model that expresses a basic phenomenology of the objective psyche, an objective paradigm against which it is possible to orient our understanding of psyche's intentions. The use of such a model was important for Jung because the alchemical corpus was seen to exceed, in richness and in scope, any individual understanding derived from case material.

On the basis of individual cases, Jung noted that one or another aspect of the individuation process tends to predominate and that the material necessarily reflects different moments of a larger view of psychic possibility. For Jung, any attempt to understand the individuation process on the basis of an individual's material alone would have to remain content with "a mosaic of bits and pieces without beginning or end" (1963, 14: 555-56). In short, alchemy for Jung helped to describe the individuation process in its "essential aspects."

Jung and Essentialism

While it is debatable whether it is at all accurate to characterize alchemy or Jung's approach as "essentialist," there has been a tendency to understand his use of archetypal material as an essentialist paradigm, insofar as he places an emphasis on a universal, fixed, and unchanging (essential) meaning. Insofar as Jung's work stresses the above, its purpose is the identification of patterns which serve to emphasize the continuities of human life from the earliest times to the present, and the structures of similarities across cultures as well. Jungians have, time and again, documented the value of such an approach, and this has become one of the identifying marks of a Jungian psychology and the import of the term "archetypal" in the classical sense. The limitation and shadow side of this emphasis is a tendency to minimize individual, cultural, and historical differences.

This shadow has brought the Jungian approach into disfavor in some quarters of our contemporary intellectual climate, and essentialism in general has been critiqued from a variety of philosophical orientations, particularly from within feminist and post-structuralist positions. It has been argued that since meaning is never completely known (a position Jung also takes), a dependence on concepts of universal and unchanging structures rather than on a plurality of individual meanings can radically miss, alter, and limit our understanding, as well as distort the subtle nuances of experience. Today's emphasis is on the particulars, and some of the above critiques go as far as challenging the concept of an essential human nature in general. It has become abundantly clear that the shadow side of essentialist thinking has led to issues of race, gender, and class oppression (Childers and Hentzi 1995, 20). This recognition has led in the direction of abandoning essentialist assumptions with a certain gain, but also with a felt loss of foundations which have served as paradigmatic. One result of this philosophical and cultural perspective is to raise the spectre of relativism with all its inherent difficulties (Edwards 1967, 3-4: 76).[1]

Subtler readings of Jung can avoid the inherent problems implicit in both a rigid essentialism and relativism. It is possible to see these positions as archetypal poles which, when split off, represent a fixation of thought. Ideally, from a Jungian point of view, these polarities represent a dynamic play in the alchemy of desire, an interplay that the analyst takes account of in the work of theory and analysis. The analyst must pay careful attention to the most personal and particular dimensions of an individual's life, gender, culture, and history, as well as how these particulars reflect and take part in the larger structural dimensions of human existence. Jungians hold a vision in which individual and archetype are interdependent and interpenetrative. When this integrated view breaks down, it can lead to splits which tend to privilege one or the other side of a false division. These splits can become metaphysical positions, and Jung never intended his thoughts to be read in that manner. David Miller (1995) comments that to see the Jungian archetype as an essentialist structure is unsophisticated and that it is by no means a metaphysical postulate. An authentically Jungian hermeneutic precisely de-essentializes meaning, rather than locating an essentialist meaning or a psychological essence (Miller 1995, 196-208).[2] Still, this essentialist perception of Jung's work remains, casting a shadow that has motivated psychological revision.

Archetypal Psychology, the Post-modern Voice, and the Alchemy of Desire

Archetypal psychology has been particularly sensitive to the essentialist shadow of Jungian psychology and how it, as well as other depth psychologies, can rigidify their metapsychological positions and become "official" statements, which, by virtue of their theory, already declare to know what the soul wants (Hillman 1983, 94). This thrust of archetypal psychology is in line with the contemporary ethos against the essentialist tendency, but seemingly unlike it, approaching the question of the soul's desire by turning directly to it through a dialogue revivifying an ancient tradition of speaking directly with the soul. Like the sacred dialogue of the Egyptian with his Ba, or Socrates with Diatoma, Hillman (1983, 86) re-engages the soul's voice following Jung's example of active imagination, privileging the alterity of voices from the background of psyche in order to hear the silence beyond the ego's speech. For Hillman, what the patient consciously says and desires is always "entangled in another factor like a thread pulling back, a reflective hesitancy which keeps assertions about what one really wants from ever finding direct speech" (1983, 85).

Hillman's reflective hesitancy, like Jacques Derrida's "gesture that hesitates between the assertive and the interrogative" (Rabaté 1994, 197), refuses the logocentrism of literal answers and refers to an unspeakable "third." For Derrida, this third is attributed to *différance*, while for Hillman, it refers to soul. *Différance* is a term coined by Derrida, indicating a condition for the possibility of meaning and is therefore presupposed by every pair of binary oppositions (Faulconer 1990, 120-21).[3] The term itself, like a true symbol in Jung's sense, resists hypostatization and remains a playful undecidable. This unspeakable third for Hillman, while never identifiable with what the ego is able to say it wants, is nevertheless "expressed" by the subtle voices of the silent speech of the unconscious. They are the subtle voices of subtle bodies, imagined voices that mark the space of consciousness with traces even as they are usually distanced, repressed, and deferred; they haunt our imagination and our dreams.

An example for me emerged when I was asked to give a lecture on psychiatry and religion. My host mentioned to me that the group would be interested in the personal experience of a Jungian analyst. When I began to write, I did so in a kind of intellectual, impersonal way and from an ego-oriented position, a kind of writing that did not particularly grip me. The writing had little soul, no images or dreams, and little of what gave dimension and value to my work. This soulless writing had no humor, no root metaphors of the kind that drive the soul toward a deepened life. That night I had a dream:

> I was invited to give a talk, it turns out to be with children.... When I started to speak I was very intellectual, abstract, and factual. As I looked out at my audience, I noticed a young boy who looked bored and pained....

As I imagined my way into the dream, I felt the little boy's response of pain and boredom to the kind of talk ego was doing. I began to pay more attention to the image of this child and wondered about what he wanted. This was a starting place that allowed me to change both my relation to him and the style and quality of my talk. It became simpler and more communicative. It was well received, and I felt a sense of gratification.

An interesting amplification and reflection on this kind of experience comes from the work of play therapy. Linney Wix notes that psychotherapy today is so progressive and heady and that "all the wordy head stuff does not impress the child. They merely want you to be present, not absent somewhere in your head" (1993, 58). This is true not only for the literal child, says Wix, but for the archetypal child as well. It demands that we take off our logical, rational hats and put on the sandals of Hermes (Sullwood 1982). This means a move from the "head place to the place of ground and matter" (Wix 1993, 58). She states that in order to do this, we would do well to retrograde to some degree, to "walk backwards," to delay our ego selves, to allow a pathway to our own unconscious. "If we do not learn this backward walk of Hermes," notes Wix, "then we are denying the place of the child, the place of soul" (1993, 60). For Wix, this movement toward the more "primitive" and "natural" is not simply regressive, but also points toward the future. The child soul in its role as a mediating symbol can unite and differentiate.

In this brief example, what the soul seemed to want differed from the ego attitude which needed to be changed to allow a fresh voice into the space of psyche. In the above, the change required less intellectual distance and a making of room for the voice of a young boy, perhaps for the voice of soul. One should be careful here not to literalize these moments in the soul's dialectic as what the soul wants in some hypostasized way, for at other moments the soul may call for intellect or other voices, the point being

simply the importance of the dialectic play of desire, the engagement with the voices on the margin of consciousness. Hillman
distills and articulates the desire of some of these other voices
from his work of active imagination, including the "desire to be
loved ... to be heard ... to be named and seen ... and to be let out of
the fiction of interiority" (1983, 127). Often, these voices of soul
are the voices of those dimensions of psyche that are kept down
and below, the inferiors, the voices of "the child, the woman, the
ancestor and the dead, the animal, the weak and hurt, the revolt-
ing and ugly, the shadows judged and imprisoned" (Hillman 1983,
113).

What seems important in all the above is to recognize there
are others, subtle voices on the fringe of consciousness that we are
called to account for and that can lead to further levels of differentiation and depth. We then speak meaningfully of a multiplicity
of intentions in the play of desire, of a dialectic of desire in which
these complex intentionalities encounter one another, where the
desire of the ego meets the desire of the shadow, anima, animus,
and other voices of the psyche. The field of desire is one in which
these differing vectors of the soul engage, rub up against one
another, collide, mesh, melt, vaporize, coagulate, differentiate and
articulate themselves in forms, patterns, dramas, stories, finding
direction and perhaps dissolving again in a cycle of the soul's
transformative experience. It is the above process that I refer to as
"the alchemy of desire."

These voices do not provide us with an overall metapsychological answer or denote a general conclusion, nor do they simply
make empirical points. Rather, they engage us in a subtle field of
traces, exchanges, and fictional enactments so that we can
develop an ear to the soul's desire. These voices, unlike the privileged speech of logocentrism, are not simply present to themselves in an unmediated way, but are part of the play of significa-
tion. They belong to a wider field of psyche (Hillman), or of signs
(Derrida). What this suggests both psychologically and linguisti-
cally is that the voice of ego or consciousness (the voice of presence) always already intends another echo or trace tacitly implied
as an aspect of the interdependence of voices in a larger dialogue.
The priority of ego's speech present to itself, thinking itself an
unmediated and direct expression, is itself an effect in a larger

context and does not simply speak, but is spoken. Derrida's decon-
structive approach, like Hillman's psychology of soul, relativises
the ego, so that the traditional historical privileging of conscious
over the unconscious, ego speech over the voice of the imaginal,
is thrown into radical questioning and paradoxical play.

In this alchemical play, the hard fast boundary of the ego is
progressively loosened and coagulated so that the clarity of binary
opposition, important at one moment, is led to a recognition of
other possibilities and to the imaginal, out of which the opposites
may diacritically engender each other in the many shades of
psyche's potential. The imaginal play of psyche itself is inarticu-
late yet spoken, inaudible yet heard, latent yet manifest, absent
yet present, and more subtly, it is out of the space between these
metaphysical opposites that the voice of desire articulates itself in
the medium where silence and expression meet. If one reads
Hillman's understanding of the imaginal voice and the image in
the above way, then the voices of archetypal psychology and post-
modern philosophy can be seen to share a medium.

The Shared Medium of Post-modernism and Archetypal Psychology: Fictional Space

For Derrida, diacritical awareness of *différance* helps to move
insight more subtly into and beyond the binary vision of metaphysical opposites, while Hillman "sees through" opposites and
reevaluates the antithetical mode of thinking:

> One is always never-only-one, but bound in a *syzygy*, a
> tandem from which ... we become able to reflect insight itself,
> to regard our own regard.... Each insight presupposes a
> perspective from which it is seen ... so when we meet the
> opposites our question will no longer be how to conjunct,
> transcend, find a synthetic third. For such moves take antithe-
> sis literally ... instead our question will be, what have we
> already done to lose our twin who was given with the soul
> (1983, 103).

This perspective shifts awareness to a field beyond opposites
to the play of the imaginal and to the realm of fictions. The
psychological space opened by post-modernism and archetypal
psychology is one that might mutually be called fiction, not in the
traditional sense of imaginary, but rather in the drawing of its

meaning from the Latin etymology of the word "fictive," indicating the capacity to shape or mold. In this space, consciousness comes to be, and with it, a sense of movement or purpose, not in the sense of known goals, but rather as guiding fictions that "show the way" (Hillman 1983, 105). Jungian and archetypal psychology speak of this directedness, "that for the sake of which" (Hillman 1993, 226) as telos, a notion that speaks directly to the question of what the soul wants, and which gets revisioned in archetypal psychology. With regard to the direction of the soul, archetypal psychology is in some respects closer to Heidegger than to Derrida: "For Heidegger, there is something like a direction ... what he calls destiny and per durance" (Faulconer 1990, 125). According to Faulconer, "It is this 'direction' or 'destination' that is the most important difference between Heidegger's and Derrida's thought":

> According to Heidegger, as a temporal being, as futural ... Dasein is *the original outside — itself.* In other words, because Dasein is essentially temporal, coming from the past and directed toward the future, it is always already beyond the moment. Or, more accurately, the moment itself is transcendental, stretching out beyond the point of the now, both backward and forward (Faulconer 1990, 125).

This odd philosophical construction, "always already beyond the moment," strange to the analyst's ear, breaks down a literal conception of temporality and opens up a new psychological space which we might relate to fictive space. It is not simply the space of being-in-time in the Heideggerian sense, but the space of soul's temporality. This would mean that time and telos can no longer simply be taken literally, but require a new understanding of the soul's way of movement and its goal.

The Revisioning of Telos and Goal

The notion of telos is revisioned in Hillman's essay on the stone. In psychological language, Hillman, like Heidegger, emphasizes circularity, repetition, reflexivity; Hillman notes that *circulatio* and *rotatio* are among the last operations of the opus (1993, 259). The *rotatio*, like a turning wheel, announces that no position can remain fixed, no statement finally true, no end place achieved. "The *rotatio* also returns telos to itself to its root meaning. *Telos* does not simply mean end, aim, goal, purpose, finis" (Hillman 1993, 259). Rather, following Onians, Hillman suggests the root meaning is a "turning around," *telos* as circling or circle (Hillman 1993, 260) (Figure 1).

Psyche's own motion is not going literally somewhere else; there is no journey outside the soul:

> The libidinal compulsion, the organic towardness of hope and desire that would always go further for a far away grail, turns around on itself and dissolves itself.... The snake eats its own tail, a goal image of deconstructive subversion" (Hillman 1983, 260).

What is accomplished in the alchemical work, according to Hillman, is a moment, "when you *awaken within the idea of the goal*, the goal is not somewhere else out there calling for attainment, but you are within the idea... " (1983, 261). Hillman's description, like a hermetic circle or Zen Satori, returns psyche to itself, to its own waters. This return sets the stage for a new understanding of the motion of the soul and of renewal.

An example of this occurred to me at a time when a dreamer was obsessed with the idea of spending time in a Tibetan monastery. He had been working on some images in the midst of his analysis, and he heard a voice from a dream the night before, which said: "you are already in a Tibetan monastery." Listening to the voice both relieved the obsession and helped him to enjoy the pleasure of working within the immediacy of his own psychic reality. This movement was not a movement away from the world and its possibilities, but rather a movement more fully into the space of the world in which he was living. It freed his imagination to see life in a larger context and left him with feelings of mystery and vitalization not unlike the feelings I described earlier in relation to the stones. It then seemed to me that his energy had been drained off by imagining life's fullness elsewhere and in the future, to a place he could go out there. The awakening within his psyche allowed him to feel an intimacy with that to which he was already connected. The bodily pleasure of this recognition was renewing a sense of archetypal *jouissance*.

Figure 1
Mercurius turning the eight-spoked wheel, which symbolizes the process.

Source: "Speculum Vegitatis" (17th century manuscript), reproduced from Jung (1953, 12: 156).

Separation and Return to Instinct and Archetypal Ground: The Process of Revivification

In our Western world, the fixation of the process of separation from our instinctual / archetypal lives has been pronounced, resulting in overly intellectualized, sublimated, and devitalized removal from ourselves and our depths. We become out of touch with our instincts, flying out into the future into the clouds vaporizing into a split-off mentalism (Figure 2). Our goals are outstretched in time ahead of us, and we become specters of ourselves in the rapid paced pursuit of progress and development in an attempt to revitalize our disembodied existence. While in the West this condition has been exaggerated, it also seems to represent a larger structural possibility of the soul.

Jung was aware of the importance of psyche's autonomy and the separation of consciousness from instinct (without which there would be no consciousness of the kind we know). He also emphasized the dangers of isolation, desolation, and unbearable alienation which the separation from instinct can cause. All these can lead to endless error and confusion (Jung 1953, 12: 131), and thus the need for rites of renewal which attempt to abolish the separation between the conscious mind and the unconscious and to bring about a reunion of the individual with his or her instinctual / archetypal make-up.

Many of Jung's cases document the soul's struggle to reconstruct a relationship to this instinctual / archetypal ground. In 1935, Jung presented one such case at Eronos and again at the Terry lectures at Yale in 1937. This case is of a man whose religious orientation was in irreconcilable conflict with what Jung called a pagan anti-ascetic tendency. The patient's attempt at spiritualization and sublimation were essentially ineffective in coming to any deep resolve. His instinctual personality had been neglected in favor of an intellectual / spiritual attitude, and his instincts were demanding his attention by attacking him in the form of uncontrollable outbursts. Jung noted that the patient was naturally afraid of these tendencies of the unconscious and that his attempts at sublimation were ineffective. Jung then suggested that what was needed was "real transformation," by which he seemed to mean something quite different than sublimation. A sublimated solution to the conflict between the man's

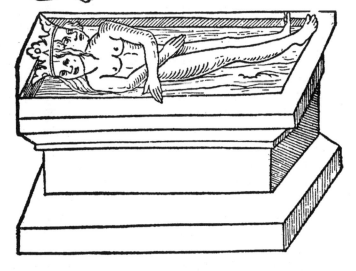

Figure 2
Extractio: The Separation of the Anima

Source: Jung (1954, 16: 269).

"Catholicism" and "pagan joie de vivre" was far too superficial, and the relationship between his spiritual and worldly attitudes was set up in a way that dulled the sharpness of his moral conflict, obscuring his deep pain and distress. This, according to Jung, resulted in a religious sentimentality instead of the numinosum of divine experience (1958, 11: 32).

Jung then reported his patient's now well-known dream, in which there is a gathering of people, a peculiar ceremony taking place, apparently of a magical character for the purpose of reconstructing a "gibbon." Jung states that the gibbon or monkey refers to the dreamer's instinctual personality which needs to be reconstructed, a prospect frightening to the dreamer, but necessary in order to undergo an important reintegration of split-off instinctuality and to bring about the transformation into a new man. Jung amplifies the gibbon image, pointing to man's archaic, bestial foundations and to the importance of the archetypal Dionysian mysteries which play an important part in rites of renewal. For Jung (1953, 129), these rites point beyond Freudian notions of regression to the archaic and infantile, to man's fundamental psychic disposition, and have been lost in our times and come closest to us in dreams. Johnson notes this loss: "It is the great tragedy of contemporary western society that we have virtually lost the ability to experience the transformative power of ecstasy and joy" (1987, vi). It is the importance of the Dionysian energy that Johnson emphasizes.

These rites are often connected to the animal, and in the above dream series, the ego must be displaced from its central role, while the center is reserved for the reconstructed gibbon, a symbol for that part of the psyche which goes down into the subhuman and yet reaches above and beyond everyday consciousness to the animal god. Jung (1953, 131) amplifies the image with the cynocephalus or dog-headed baboon associated with Thoth-Hermes, the highest among the apes known to the Egyptians (Figure 3).

In Jung's experience, the conscious mind, as we know it, can only claim a relatively central position and must put up with the fact that the unconscious psyche transcends and, as it were, surrounds it on all sides, connecting it backwards with physiological states, on the one hand, and the archetypal dimension, on the other (1953, 132). Hillman (1977, 43) forwards Jung's examination of the monkey and its archetypal relevance, noting both the importance of the restoration of the beast and yet the incredible danger in doing so. He warns of the importance of "how the assimilation takes place: whether it be for the sake of humanity or for bestiality" (Hillman 1977, 43). With the monkey comes an ambivalence of madness and the wisdom of nature, the deepest shadow of prehistoric man, and his highest potential (Figure 4).

For Jung and Hillman, the assimilation takes us deeply into the ambivalences of the shadow, a return which is necessary if fallen man is to restore his divine likeness. For both, our period of history calls up the ape as a compensation to the ego-centricity of our time, requiring the return of the monkey into the foreground. Hillman observes the importance of this figure in its archetypal form in the work of the alchemist Robert Fludd, who also placed the ape in the center of his cosmic mandala, showing the relationship between man, nature, and heaven (Figure 5). Picasso, in his late paintings, also depicted the return of the monkey as a chthonic force of the psyche, which Jung saw in terms of the journey through the psychic history of mankind and which had as its object the restoration of the whole man (Hillman 1977, 43).[4]

The Dream as Access to the Soul's Desire — a Mosaic of Bits and Pieces without Beginning or End: Clinical Vignettes

The appearance of the monkey in our time continues in the dreams of contemporary patients expressing the soul's desire for wholeness, to reconnect with their instinctual and archetypal ground. Dreams as the soul's mirror offer us a unique view into the alchemy of desire, into its particular complexity. While for Jung, individual examples drawn from case material are limited to a "mosaic of bits and pieces," and cannot demonstrate the "essential nature" of the individuation process, he and other clinicians nonetheless offer us, through individual example, the precise way in which our essential human possibilities are actualized and inscribed in their particular uniqueness. The gathering of these examples constitutes an analytic lore and reference, demonstrating our healing fictions. As a whole, these particular stories of the soul's desire mark with poetic precision a range of metaphors of transformation, from the more common to the margins of our

Figure 3
Thoth as Cynocephalus (XXth dynasty), 12th century BCE in the
Hahnlooser Collection, Bern.

Source: Jung (1953, 12: 131).

Figure 4
Demon in the shape of a monkey — "Speculum humanae
salvationis" (Codex Latin 511, Paris, 14th century)

Source: Jung (1953, 12: 130).

Figure 5
The anima mundi, guide of mankind -- engraving by J.T. de Bry,
from Fludd, Utriusque cosmi (1617).

Source: Fabricius (1976, 46).

analytic experience.

Gene Monick, a Jungian colleague, related an interesting monkey dream to me. The following dream took place at the closure of his analytic training in Zurich. This dream seemed to me a compelling image of the "crowning of matter" and instinct:

> I am a medical student present at a pathology demonstration in medical school. The male cadaver, with an open abdomen, is on an operating table and we students, probably twenty of us, are standing behind a rope barrier watching the professor demonstrate how one ascertains the cause of death.
>
> He reaches behind himself and pulls out a one thousand pound gorilla, placing it next to the body. The gorilla begins to eat the viscera from the body. The professor says that he knows the cause of death when the gorilla gets ill from eating a diseased organ. I push to the front of the students to see better. I am fascinated.
>
> The gorilla then reaches up into the thoracic cavity of the cadaver and pulls out a tiny baby monkey, perhaps eight to ten inches long, as though he were delivering it at birth. Then a flight of golden steps descends over the table, and the gorilla ascends the steps, holding the baby monkey in its palm, places the monkey on a throne at the top of the steps, and places a crown upon its head. I am spellbound.

Monick presented the dream to his supervisors in the final session with them. They are reported to have said to the candidate: "Monick, your god is a monkey. Forget everything you learned here. Go back and practice with your instinct and intuition."[5] While this example of the emergence of the animal into the foreground is anecdotal and not meant to exemplify an analysis of the dream or even the full context of exchange, it does resonate with the significant recognition of the monkey as an important archetypal figure for our time.

The next clinical vignette echoes this story, as well as Jung's example of the gibbon image, while offering a contemporary variation on the theme. It is from the analysis of a successful businessman who, while having wide-ranging creative and spiritual energies, was struggling to make room for them in his everyday life. He had been losing his energy for pursuing the same professional demands that had made him successful. He had a strong moral conscience, but had difficulty with some shadow issues and with integrating both his sexual and spiritual needs. He had felt for some time there was something else his soul desired, but was not sure what it was. He was having a hard time making room for what he thought could help him reorient and renew his life. He had fantasized about allowing four hours each morning to read, meditate, and work on his dreams, feeling these activities would be a good balance. Even though his financial situation would allow for this and he consciously wanted it, something stood in the way of making a significant enough adjustment in his situation. He then had the following dream:

> He is with a small group of three or four men. They went to the edge of a pond where a monster was supposedly living. They played music for four hours in an attempt to awaken the monster. He remembers either telling them or thinking to himself this was not a good idea. They started to return to the city, leaving the woods behind where the pond was located. They had not stirred the monster. Apparently, as they got closer to the edge of town in the distance from the woods where the pond was, a huge King Kong-like creature was stalking. Everyone in the city started to flee as the creature approached. Musicians, who were friends of his, started to head underground to hide. He thought they would be better off hiding above ground, where they could avoid being cornered, although at the risk of being more visible. He thought, but was not sure, that he jumped down into the crowd going underground. King Kong roamed through the city, crushing buildings. He remembers coming out from hiding after days had passed. People were in mass confusion (massa confusa), with little law and order. [The patient is a person who always follows the rules.]

> He then found food at a sandwich vendor's stand. Everyone with him just took sandwiches without paying, even though the vendor was there. Later, at the end of the dream, he and his friends realize that King Kong had not hurt anyone even though he had been roaming the area for many days. He then realized that perhaps the ape was good and was actually there to befriend and help them. He also discovered that a very

small white bird moved in advance of him at a given distance.
He saw the bird outside and tried to communicate with it,
that perhaps it was an advance messenger, some sort of intermediary with whom he could communicate and, through it,
learn about King Kong. As he approached the bird and King
Kong, King Kong would be roused, but if he stayed on the
other side of the bird, such that the bird was between them,
King Kong could not be roused. He tested this by stepping
back and forth over the place where the bird was. He then realized that he was dancing with the bird and that it was an intermediary, and also that King Kong was a very sensitive, huge
force that was there to help.

The final image of the monster was of an extremely large,
colorful creature sitting in a sphinx-like posture.

While an exhaustive analysis of this dream is not possible in
this context, I would like to make a few observations. The
dreamer feels himself to be somewhat alienated from his instinctual life, at times feeling that he is not in his life vitally, but
instead observing it from behind a glass shield. His soul seems to
desire a reconnection with his depths and a vitalization of his life.

The dream begins with a constellation of the masculine
psyche and a going to the edge of a certain depth, under which
something felt to be monstrous is living. Yet there seems to be an
ambivalent desire to awaken it, calling it forth in a time frame
(four hours), concordant with the dreamer's waking fantasy of the
time he needs, but is having difficulty taking. In the dream, the
call of music at first seems to bear no results, and the dream ego
is feeling some concern about awakening this force. Suddenly, the
big ape-like energy awakens and causes panic, fear for his life, and
the desire to hide. Certain structures are crushed, and *massa
confusa* results with the breakdown of law and order. After that,
the dream ego finds itself breaking rules, taking nourishment
without paying (something the waking ego would never do).
Consciously, the patient is a very moral, law-abiding man to a
fault. After this breakdown and breakout, the dream ego has a new
observation — that although this powerful energy has been
released for some time, it really has not hurt anyone — and the
idea dawns that it may not be a bad force, but instead be a good
one which is there to befriend.

The possibility of communicating with this energy emerges by virtue of a certain spirit which flies out in advance, as an intermediary between the dream ego and the ape-like entity. The dreamer then begins to experiment with how close he can get to it, seeking to find a proper relationship, moving closer and retreating, in a dance-like fashion. As he moves in relation to this energy, he begins to feel that the ape is a very sensitive creature and may have even come to help. This, then, seems to open the way for a new appearance of this huge energy as a multicolored, highly differentiated mystery, a riddle of the soul which presents itself as if to ask an important question. What began as a terrible fear of being overwhelmed by the Dionysian psyche threatening an enantiodromia emerges as something which, while crushing old structures, also allows a new relationship to the mysterious, highly differentiated mysteries of psyche with which the ego can have a relationship.

It is not surprising that the patient had a good deal of resistance to this archetypal energy, fearing that given a little room, it could destroy everything. This is the danger and the promise of the wild man archetype. It is interesting to notice the parallels not only with Jung's patient, but also with Robert Bly's (1990) elaboration of the *Iron John* story, in which there is a large man covered with hair from head to foot. For Bly, this wild man lies at the bottom of the psyche of every modern man. Making contact with him is the step that every modern man has to make, according to Bly. For the man who has the courage to go down to the bottom of the pond, it is a step surrounded with fear even more so now that "corporations do so much work to produce the sanitized, hairless, shallow man.... For generations now, the industrial community has warned young businessmen to keep away from *Iron John* and the Christian Church is not fond of him either" (Bly 1990, 6).

Whatever one thinks of Bly's scathing critique, it seems to follow, psychologically, that the more removed we become from our primitive and instinctual nature, the more frightening it becomes, and the more it is desired and needed by the soul. Welcoming the hairy man is risky and requires a willingness to descend into the depths of the male psyche and "accept what's dark down there" (Bly 1990, 6). This is the kind of activation that occurred in the above patient, and his approaching the depths enlivened his primitive energies. His dream laid out the potential for descending and accepting this deeper mystery.

In the following dream, the patient was back at college and walking along the sidewalk when he heard music, a fast-paced ethnic jig. He decided to dance in an almost involuntary way with joy and excitement. His feet moved quickly back and forth (like his dance with the bird). Then he approached some steps and went down. This archetypal step is amplified by Hillman who, quoting Jung, says that, "the journey through the psychic history of mankind has as its object, the restoration of the whole man — (and that), it is upon the `essentially primitive creature' that the *kairos* depends" (Hillman 1979, 43). Hillman, like Jung, sees this primitive creature as having a divine quality which is always based upon an animal. For Hillman (1979, 47), to remain human requires maintaining a connection with this animal, with the subhuman, remaining true to one's shadow and to the madness which is, as well, the wisdom of nature, that is, the unconscious itself. Ape as familiaris, guide, and companion means reintegrating some of what has been split off by the nineteenth century religious view of man (Hillman 1979, 48). It is a return to the all too human, which has been buried or cast behind us in our climb to the light. From our rarified position, what is left behind looks too much like a monkey, "too hairy, too embarrassing, too tricky and (oddly) too wise" (Hillman 1979, 44).

To live with our central axis represented by the ape's folly, anarchy, and vice is always to be hearing his music, to have our ear to the shadow/angel. This is to remain in contact with the subhuman, yet divine, center (Hillman 1979, 47). A return to this archetypal energy is not a transcendence of good and evil, but a staying within these opposites and an integrating of them from below (Hillman 1979, 48). For Hillman, quoting Jung, this means remaining within the tension of ambivalence, "where the gods are symbolized by animals, where the holy ghost is a bird, and the wise old man is a big ape" (Hillman 1979, 44). At the end of the dream described above, we leave our patient with the animal (the higher ape?) seen in a new light, in a multicolored mystery, and with the bird messenger as a link to what does seem to be a carrier of instinctual wisdom.

The relationship with this emerging energy and descent to its depths can be seen in an alchemical image, taken from the Rosarium, entitled *Reviving* (Figure 6). This descent, which depicts the soul's return to the material body, is also a vitalization and "revivification." It is a way of imagining what the soul wants and is a relinking with the body and the world. It is a relinking to the instinctual / archetypal lived body — animal, erotic, and sacred. It is the moment where the soul descends from heaven, "beautiful and glad" (Hillman 1993, 264). The soul yearns to enjoy this world and "has as its goal a resurrection in beauty and plea-sure" (Hillman 1993, 261). For Hillman, resurrection of the ape is likewise a resurrection of the libido, an erotic power which heralds the alchemical rubedo, the vital reddening of life. With the reddening comes the enlivening that the patient described above was missing and which began to show itself as his world began to be colored. The image of the red stone was one of the important images of the goal for alchemy, a vision of the perfection of the stone and a crowning and exultation of matter (Hillman 1993, 264-65).

Fire in the Stone: A Ruby Dream

The final dream and clinical vignette centers on an image of the red stone and is from a young man at the beginning of his third year in analysis. He grew up in a fundamentalist religious family and, although he was consciously separated from their values, unconscious connections continued to bind him. He was in a posi-tion below his level of talent and creativity, and his soul yearned for something more. Yet he had trouble seeking a fuller life and a position more commensurate with his potential. He involved himself in a number of relationships with women, but often felt unappreciated and undervalued; in addition, he undervalued himself in spite of some considerable gifts. He was able, in the course of our work, to have a productive relationship with the unconscious which roared below the surface of his conscious adaptation, and at the time of this dream, he was feeling the need to make a move in his life. He was bored with work and drawn to new possibilities about which he was ambivalent, yet very excited.

He is at work in his office, and all the furniture has been removed from it. The carpet on the floor is different. He

Figure 6
Revivication: The Return of Anma

Source: Jung (1954, 285).

thinks it is a new rug: it is loosened at the ends and is blowing up. He hears a deep roar from down below from the ventilation system. Then an Indian woman appears to him; he is not sure why she is there. He doesn't know whether she is an employee, but doesn't think so. She has a wide face and large, deep black eyes. She is beautiful in an exotic way. He starts to approach her, fearing he may be moving too fast or being too forward. He lays her down on the carpet and realizes below the carpet is a grate, and he hears a low roar coming from underneath. It is the main ventilation duct, which has been thinly veiled by the carpet. He begins to run his hand up her thigh to find she has a gold clip covering her clitoris. The clip is ornate, and at her vaginal opening, there is a large ruby rock so she cannot have intercourse. He is freaked out by this, but remembers she is from a different culture. He wonders about her being clean because the clip on her clitoris reminds him of bondage and prostitution.

Again, while a more complete analysis is not possible here, there are a number of useful elaborations of this dream that forward our reflection on what the soul appears to want. Taking up the dream with this question in mind leads us to recall the patient's feeling of boredom with his work and the need to move on. One might imagine his soul as feeling empty in the place of work. What made him feel comfortable there is gone — the furniture has been removed. Something new is on the ground and there is a loosening, a spirit is blowing up. He hears something down below: it is a ventilation system — a system that carries the flow of air or spirit. One gets a sense at the beginning of this dream of the inner vision of the outer situation — of the soul's emptying out, of its new covering, of its loosening, and of the flow of its spirit.

As the patient considers leaving his current job, he is undergoing a movement which seems to lay the ground for the appearance of this exotic woman (anima). He is not sure why she is there, but whatever she represents, he is interested. In his analytic exploration of this image, he reflected on his sense that she was not an employee, and he realizes that he doesn't want to be an employee either. She is broader, deeper, and different than this ego identification. He lays her down on new ground, only to discover that something is blocking both her pleasure and his entering her as well. What blocks his entry is a large red ruby.

This situation sets up a certain complexity of the soul. The dreamer seems to want to enter into her directly, but he is confronted with an impasse, and so begins the alchemy of desire. The desire to enter in rubs up against a stone. A first exploration of this stone revealed an interesting and rather startling association: that the ruby is his birth stone. Why, we wondered, would his birth stone stand in the way of entering into this new, exotic possibility? A first level of exploration revealed a number of associations to his past, to his birth "rite." Coming from a fundamentalist religious background on his mother's side made it clear that seeking money and material success, as well as pleasure, was not only frowned upon, but was in the worst case scenario, "working with the devil." In this way, the patient's unconscious connection to his mother inhibited his soul's desire to seek out new possibilities since to do so would be dirty and resemble prostitution. However, the dream ego had enough differentiation to hold such negative judgment in relative suspension. This woman might be more than a prostitute because she is from another culture and has a more mysterious sense about her. Nevertheless, the issue of money was a block to him, both desired and tabooed, and it created a sado-masochistic position in which it blocked and promised pleasure at the same time. A gold clip (money holder) covered and marked the place of pleasure.

All of our piecing together of historical material made sense to the dreamer. He even remembered that before his mother had joined her religious sect, things were different. He felt that she was then very sensitive to him, and he recalled a time when she had given him a small bag of polished stones, one of which was a small ruby. This was very important to him, marking the time before his mother transformed her life by entering into a fundamentalist religious sect. The patient felt some nostalgia and grief for the mother he had lost. This memory made sense of the patient's desire to return to the experience of his mother before her change — to enter into her and reexperience the pleasure of her "bejeweled body" — but this experience was blocked. This interpretation, while ringing true to the dreamer, also felt limited. He felt that the stone and the woman of his dream had a more mysterious meaning and he wasn't satisfied. He stated that the dream ruby was not the one his mother had given him and, as much as he could identify the maternal longings, they were qualitatively different from what this mysterious woman seemed to hold out.

We returned once again to the stone, drawing forth further possibilities that seemed to complement, amplify, and deepen what we had arrived at to this point. In describing the stone, he stated:

> A ruby comes out of the earth, and when it does, it's nothing special. It comes out of a very rough, dirty mine or somehing. It takes somebody with knowledge about what they are really looking for to bring it into its fullness.

He reflected: "In some way, I guess I come from a dirty, rough place and through others and myself, I was able to form into what I was meant to be." I stated to him that he had, indeed, come through a lot and that now he had a many-faceted nature and was cut beautifully, and that others valued him. This released a good bit of sadness.

One could say that I was mirroring the patient in a way that recaptured a maternal mirroring that he was longing for and felt blocked from. In a sense, this seems right, yet I have come to feel with the patient that what is getting mirrored is more mysterious, and that the deeper "mirroring" is accomplished by the specificity of the image and the dream. It is through reflection on the image that the patient was able to arrive at the experience of what the soul wanted — a sense of recognition of his difficult journey, of what he had been through and coming to be what he was meant to be. The more positive sense of self which he may have experienced and anticipated as a child was now carried in the soul in a stone of many facets, in the reddening of this desire, in his buried potential held by the feminine. In the stone was a more exalted sense of being. By further imagining himself into the stone, the patient stated that it felt elemental, and that he, as stone, felt polished, centered, more powerful, attractive, and coveted. In reflecting on the above, he realized how he never allowed himself to think or feel these thoughts, could not enter them. In this way, his soul's desire was blocked, but through the image, he was now moving toward his buried potential.[6]

If Jung is correct that the Self is not an introject, but is itself projected onto our earliest experiences of the parental imagos, then the stone as a mirror reflects not simply the mother, but what the mother originally carried that belonged to the patient that is his stone. His birthstone was the carrier of the inextinguishable flame that was there at the beginning, and which for a while was promised to him through his relationship with mother. The differentiation distinguishes the personal from the archetypal transference and suggests that the mirror of transference is carried not simply in the analyst, but in the image — image as mirror transference to the archetypal potentials of the soul. In my patient's dream, this potential is carried by an exotic woman whose reddened stone is held in the genitals, keeping the image of the self from appearing simply as a sublimated spiritual value.

Interestingly, as well, the red stone was one of the important images of the goal of western and eastern alchemy. Katon Shual (1995, 45) has linked the notion of the philosopher's stone as first matter to the eastern concept of Rasa, noting that *Rasaratnakara* means making a jewel of Rasa.[7] While referring to the stone, Rasa also refers to the essence of bodily fluids, especially to those secreted by the body when sexually aroused, as well as to the emotional and aesthetic sentiments that are part of the act of love. In this image, sexuality and divinity are intimately intertwined. Shual notes that in magical practices, partners make a dedication in the sacred space of the circle, and the genitals are seen as visible representations of the divine. One of the tasks of this initiation is the discovery of the esoteric doctrine of the body.

In light of this amplification, it is interesting to consider the notion that the "esoteric body" is also a libidinized body that, according to Hillman, maintains an Aphroditic quality, which serves to maintain a sensate attraction to the goal, "as a pleasurable pull toward beauty."[8] Voluptas, according to Apuleius, "lies curled in the womb of Psyche" (Hillman 1993, 262-63) and, like our red stone, is contained by the exotic otherness of the self, a reddened mirror of the soul.

Hillman makes an imaginal corelation that connects our last two dream examples, linking the libidinized stone with the resurrection of the ape, seeing in both a material "generative erotic power which reddens into life" (1993, 164, 263). Both images lead

to an exaltation, which Martin Ruland's (1964) alchemical dictionary defines as an operation by which a matter is altered in its
inclinations and is elevated to a higher dignity of substance and
virtue (Hillman 1993, 265). My patient certainly felt an elevated
sense of dignity and substance as he felt mirrored in the stone. His
reddening had not changed his story, but revealed it to him in a
way he could not see without the stone. His story was what it
was, but could now be seen in a larger perspective, and he could
appreciate having made the journey. At the end of the analysis, he
shared the following from his diary:

> In the three years that I was in analysis, I worked on my exter-
> nally formative problems such as my alcoholic father,
> passively controlling mother, a cataclysmic religion, and the
> shame of growing up in a poor neighborhood, only as a back-
> drop to the much bigger internal world. The analysis was
> really not about solving problems as much as it was an oppor-
> tunity to value and appreciate a much larger and diverse sense
> of the self. It was a discovery which made the suffering of the
> past somehow just part of the bigger picture, rather than the
> focus. The unwitting benefit of hardship is that it builds char-
> acter and soul. I didn't particularly want to be building char-
> acter as a twelve-year-old forced into stepping into my father's
> absent shoes with the weight of God's damnation upon me,
> but beyond the pathology of that role lies someone who with-
> stood the storms and invariably came out a better and wiser
> sailor.

Hillman, describing the reddening, states that it does not
mean that something is transcended and spiritualized, but rather
that a nobler notion of matter prevails. Matter is crowned, and
thereby its virtues are revealed and its inclinations alter from
being the "lodestone of dumb, concrete daily obstruction to the
ruby rocks that provide our life with daily pleasure" (Hillman
1993, 265).

Conclusion

The above exploration was not intended to prove or demonstrate
any particular conclusion, but rather to inquire into the questions
of psyche's intention. Through reflection and examples, the hope
is that these bits and pieces amplify our analytic lore and show

how the soul seems to exhibit a creative direction. In this regard, our inquiry followed post-modern and archetypal sensibilities which suggest some revisioning of our traditional concepts of telos and goal and, together, open the notion of a fictional space in which an alchemy of desire is enacted, emphasizing particular images of the soul's intention. Images such as the monkey and the stone, while having archetypal significance, function in a very particular way in each context and are best read with a non-essentialist eye.

Notes

1 Relativism as a general philosophical idea that is understood in a variety of ways can refer to the relativity of knowledge as functionalism, historicism, skepticism, or ethical relativism. Not all relativistic theories are simply equatable with subjectivism. What is implied here is the experience of a loss of foundations, of absolutes, of universals, and of basic structures — the struggles that ensue with this breakdown (Edwards 1967, 3-4: 76).

2 The developmental perspective in Jungian psychology also shares with archetypal psychology a sensitivity to the shadow of essentialism in Jungian thought. I have chosen to emphasize the archetypalist approach since I think it is more radical and in tune with the ethos of the contemporary intellectual trends. The developmental approach, while also less subject to the shadow of essentialism, often loses the archetypal perspective and remains rooted in a traditional subject-object dichotomy and in an ego psychology.

3 Faulconer explains:

> The point of Derrida's discussion of différance (a neologism and one among several names he uses for what he is talking about), is to show the origin of systems in difference (the "space" between the elements or threads of any system), and deferral (the deferral of any "last word," of any metaphysical resolution in the transcendent, of any final re-presentation) — in play, if play is conceived not as arbitrariness, but as give and take.
>
> Classically philosophy has dealt with binary differences — being and nothingness, space and time, plenitude and emptiness, true and false, sameness and otherness, male and female. However, one or another member of these sets of dyads has always held the upper hand, has always been the origin in terms of which the other was

discussed: being has been taken to be a more fundamental concept than nothingness, space more than time, plenitude more than emptiness, true more than false, sameness more than otherness, and male more than female. In each case, one of the elements of these pairs has been made fundamental, has been privileged, and while the other has been explained in terms of it. In each case, one of these elements is the presence (the transcendent) we make manifest in expression and explanation, and the other element is supposedly made absent.

Such privileging of one element of a pair idealizes closure, bringing explanation (and, indeed, all discourse) to a halt if the privileged element succeeds in taking on the ontological status of the medieval God, the unchanging source of all being. Any adequate explanation would re-present the unchanging source fully; it would no longer need to be spoken. Nothing more could be said once the adequate explanation was given; continued explanation would merely mark a previous failure to explain adequately.

Thus, on this traditional, privileging view, the end of thinking and explanation is absolute silence, the silence of a god who needs no longer to speak, for everything has been said (1990, 120-21).

Faulconer goes on to define *différance* as,

... the space between the pairs of the metaphysical tradition, and deferral, the deferral of the final presencing promised by privileging one element of those pairs — [différance] accounts for the necessity of continued speaking. The space between the pairs is the space from which any presence springs, the space from which any privileging of one thing over another is possible. Presence is not a result only of the privileged term itself. It is a result of the play of the elements, a play that makes the elements, as elements of metaphysical pairs, possible. Because the elements of the pairs exist only in play with one another, the privileging of one element always carries with it the denied member of the pair; the denied member insinuates itself in every re-presentation of the privileged member (1990, 121).

4 A number of Picasso's monkey drawings are contained in Cox and Povey (1995, 163-71).

5 Personal letter with thanks for the dream and permission to publish to Gene Monick.

6 It is an interesting amplification to note that the ruby has many names in Sanskrit, some of them clearly showing that the Hindus valued it more than any other gem. For instance, it is called *ratnaraj*, "king of precious stones." The glowing hue of the ruby suggested the idea that an inextinguishable flame burned in this stone. From this fancy comes the assertion

that the inner fire could not be hidden as it would shine through the clothing or through any material that might be wrapped around the stone. See Kunz (1913, 101).

7 Shual links the Indian alchemical and Tantrik traditions together.

8 Hillman emphasizes the importance of sensuous content, noting the word libido belongs to a word cluster including libation, as pouring of liquid, *deliquore* (to make liquid, meet), *laetus* (moist, fat, fruitful, glad), and the German *lieben* or love, as well as *liaber* (free). The God liber, the procreative fertility figure.

Bibliography

Bly, Robert. 1990. *Iron John*. Woburn, Massachusetts: Addison-Wesley Publishing Co., Inc.

Childers, Joseph and Gary Hentzi, ed. 1995. *Dictionary of Modern Literary and Cultural Criticism*. New York: Columbia University Press.

Cox, Neil and Deborah Povey. 1995. *A Picasso Bastiary*. London: Academy Editions.

Edinger, Edward. 1985. *The Anatomy of the Psyche*. La Salle, Illinois: Open Court.

Edwards, Paul, ed. 1967. *Encyclopedia of Philosophy* 3-4.

Fabricius, Johannes. 1976. *Alchemy: The Medieval Alchemists and Their Royal Art*. Copenhagen: Rosenkilde and Bagger.

Faulconer, James. 1990. "Heidegger and Psychological Explanation: Taking Account of Derrida." In *Reconsidering Psychology Perspectives from Continental Philosophy*, edited by J.E. Faulconer and R.N. Williams. Pittsburgh: Duquesne University Press.

Hillman, James. 1979. "Senex and Puer." In *Puer Papers*. Section 8. Irving, Texas: Spring Publications.

——. 1983. *Healing Fiction*. Barrytown, New York: Station Hill Press.

——. 1993. "Concerning the Stone: Alchemical Images of the Goal." *Sphinx 5, London Convivium for Archetypal Studies*. London.

Johnson, H. Robert. 1987. *Ecstasy*. San Francisco: Harper and Row.

Jung, C.G. 1953. *Psychology and Alchemy*. *Collected Works* 12 Princeton, New Jersey: Pantheon Books.

———. 1954. *The Practice of Psychotherapy. Collected Works* 16. New York: Bollingen Foundation and Pantheon Books.

———. 1956. *Symbols of Transformation. Collected Works* 5. Princeton, New Jersey: Princeton University Press and Bollingen Foundation.

———. 1958. *Psychology and Religion: West and East. Collected Works* 11. Princeton, New Jersey: Pantheon Books.

———. 1963. *Mysterium Coniunctionis. Collected Works* 14. Princeton, New Jersey: Pantheon Books.

Kunz, George Frederich. 1913. *The Curious Lore of Precious Stones.* Philadelphia and London: Lippincott.

McLean, Adam, ed. 1980. *The Rosary of the Philosophers.* Edinburgh: Magnum Opus Hermetic Sourceworks, no. 6.

Miller, David, ed. 1995. *Jung and the Interpretation of the Bible.* New York: Continium.

Rabaté, Jean Michal. 1994. *The Johns Hopkins Guide to Literary Theory and Criticism,* edited by M. Groden and M. Kreiswirth. Baltimore and London: John Hopkins University Press.

Shual, Katon. 1995. *Sexual Magick.* Oxford: Mandrake Press.

Sullwood, Edith. 1982. "Treatment of Children in Analytical Psychology." In *Jungian Analysis,* edited by Murray Stein, 235-55. Boston: Shambhala.

Wix, Linney. 1993. "Hermes and His Tricks in the Child Therapy Relationship." *International Journal of Play Therapy* 2, no. 1: 49-62.

Chapter 2

The Seduction of Black[1]

James Hillman

The principal of the art is the raven ...
(Jung 1963, 14: paragraph 36).

The Color of Non-Color

Black and White — these two non-colors to the Newtonian eye of science are, to the eye of culture, the first of all colors — the truly primary colors.

University of California ethnologists published a survey of the words for colors in some ninety-eight languages (Berlin and Kay 1969). From this base, they made a wider, universal claim, reporting that all languages have terms for black and white, dark and light, obscure and bright. Furthermore, they reported that if a language has a third color term, it is universally red; and if a fourth and fifth, it is universally yellow or green; followed by blue; sixth, it is brown; seventh; and so on — a scale that operates almost without exception in their collection of diverse languages.

For us, their principal finding, and the one least contested by others, is the primacy of the black-white pair. All cultures, it seems, make this distinction, this fact suggesting the importance of the diurnal rhythm (Durand 1963) and, particularly for psychology, that contrast is essential to consciousness.

Among sub-Saharan African peoples, the three primary colors — black, white, and red (and I am translating more metaphorically concrete expressions into our abstract color terms) — form the very ruling principles of the cosmos. They are not merely color words, names of hues. We find a similar idea in the three gunas in Indian cosmology: black *tamas*, red *rajas*, and white *sattva* enter into the composition of all things. The deservedly authoritative anthropologist Victor Turner (1967) states that these three colors, "provide a primordial classification of reality." They are not merely perceptual qualities, but as "experiences common to all mankind," they are like archetypal "forces," "biologically, psychologically, and logically prior to social classifications, moieties, clans, sex totems, and all the rest." For culture, black and white, as well as red, precede and determine the way human life is lived.

Turner's claim further separates the "culture" of color from the "science" of color. From the cultural viewpoint, colors are not mere secondary qualities, reducible to physical sensations in neurological systems in the subjective perceiver. On the one hand, colors have to do with light, reflection, optics, and nerves; on the other hand, they have something to do with the world itself. They are the world itself, and this world is not merely a colored world, as if by accidents of light and chemistry, or as if decorated by a painterly God. Colors present the world's phenomenal actuality — the way the world shows itself — and, as operational agents in the world, colors are primary formative principles. Even the rainbow derives its colors from the phenomenal world (rather than from the refraction of light) according to the mediaeval imagination: "From the heavens it derives the fiery color; from water, the purple; from air, the blue; and from the earth the grassy color" (Boyer 1987).

Whether the earth takes its colors from an invisible, colorless light above or composes that light by means of its own elemental hues (green grass, blue water), the rainbow joins visible and invisible. The Torah says God set forth the rainbow as a visible sign that the cosmos is sustained by invisible principles. The rainbow also declares the double principle that the display of beauty goes hand in hand with discrimination, the spectrum of finely differentiated hues.

Only in a physically reduced world view, a world view reduced to, and by, physics, can black be called a non-color, an absence of color, a deprivation of light. This privative definition of black ignores the fact that black appears in broad daylight in naturally given pigments and in other phenomena, from charcoal and obsidian to blackberries and animal eyes.

Moreover, the negative and primitive definition of black promotes the moralization of the black-white pair. Black, then, is defined as NOT-white and is deprived of all the virtues attributed to white. The contrast becomes opposition, even contradiction, as if day would be defined as non-night, and a blackberry be defined as a non-whiteberry. The law of contradiction, when moralized, gives rise to our current Western mindset, beginning in the sixteenth and seventeenth centuries — the Age of Light — where God is identified with whiteness and purity, and black, with the *privatio boni*, becoming ever more strongly the color of evil.

Northern European and American racism may have begun in the moralization of color terms. Long before any English-speaking adventurer touched the shores of West Africa, fifteenth-century meanings of "black" included: "deeply stained with dirt; soiled; foul; malignant, atrocious, horrible, wicked; disastrous, baneful, sinister...." When the first English-speaking sailors spied natives on West African shores, they called these people "black." That was the first generally descriptive term they used — not naked, not savage, not pagan — but black. Once named, these native peoples carried all the meanings implied in that term. The English term "white" to characterize an ethnic group first occurs in 1604, after the perception of Africans as "black." The moralization and opposition between white and black continues to this day in general English language usage, as white equals good, and black equals bad, dirty, foul, sinister, and evil. "White" as a term for Christians had become firmly established by 1680 in the American lexicon.

Disdain for black is not only contemporary, Western, and English. The color black in the Greek world, and in African languages also, carried meanings contrasting with white and red, and included not only the fertility of the earth and the mystery of the underworld, but also disease, suffering, labor, sorcery, and bad luck.

Black, however, is no more cursed than any other color. In fact, color terms bear extremely contrary meanings. Each is weighted down with a composite of opposites — yellow with sunshine and decay; green with hope and envy; blue with puritanism and prurience. The curse of black comes only when color terms are laid onto human beings, a curse of our Anglo-American culture and, as I have tried elsewhere at length to explain,[2] a curse that has plagued the majority culture by labelling it white, thereby loading it with the archetypal curse of white supremacy.

Could there be an archetypal aspect to darkness that might account for our disdain, as well as the fear, the physiological shudder, it can release? Does the human eye prefer light to darkness? Is the human being heliotropic, fundamentally adapted to light? Is visual perception its preferred sense, as we witness in the embryo, where from its earliest weeks, the rudimentary optical system begins to form before many others?

If the human animal has an innate predilection to light, then the exclusion of black as a color term substituting for "darkness" might find justification. The exclusion of darkness favors adaptation to the phenomenal world and optimal functioning within it by means of our primary organs of sense — the eyes. Then, we might conclude that the definition of black as a non-color belongs to the ocular identity of human consciousness. The eye becomes the *pars pro toto* for habitual human consciousness, and black threatens the very core of this identity.

The Alchemical Nigredo

The cosmic significance of these three primary colors appears as well in early Western science, that is, in the tradition of alchemy. Of the three, black plays an especially important role as the base of the work and even enters into the formation of the word "alchemy." The root, *khem*, refers to Egypt as the "black land," or land of black soil, and the art of alchemy was called a "black" art or science. The Western alchemical tradition traces its source to the *techne* of Egyptian embalming, dyeing of cloth, jewelry, and cosmetics.

The first four color terms — black, white, red, and yellow — are also the primary color terms embracing the entire alchemical opus — *nigredo, albedo, xanthosis* or *citrinitas*, and *rubedo*. These color terms describe: (1) stages of the work, (2) conditions of the material worked on, and (3) states in the psyche of the artifex or worker-alchemist. Each color term combines three distinct categories which our modern consciousness keeps separate: the mode of working, the stuff worked on, and the condition of the worker. For our epistemology, there is no inherent or necessary relation among method, problem, and subjectivity.

For example, for any substance to enter the *nigredo* phase and blacken, the operations must be dark and are called, in alchemical language, *mortificatio, putrefactio, calcinatio,* and *iteratio.* That is, the modus operandi is slow, repetitive, difficult, desiccating, severe, astringent, effortful, coagulating, and/or pulverizing. All the while, the worker enters a *nigredo* state: depressed, confused, constricted, anguished, and subject to pessimistic, even paranoid, thoughts of sickness, failure, and death.

The alchemical mode of science maintained the law of similitudes among all participants in any activity: the work, the way of working, and the worker. All must conform, whereas we can have a science in which the subjectivity of the experimenter may be radically separated from the experimental design and from the materials of the experiment.

Our science seeks a universality of experimental design that can be used by any worker, anywhere, on any problem. Statistics are, therefore, essential to it. Alchemical method, by contrast, treats each problem by each alchemist according both to its nature and to his or her nature. That is why no comprehensive system can be drawn from alchemical texts; why measurement plays an indifferent role; why the inventions of each alchemist are stridently opposed by other alchemists; and why even the materials worked on are so radically differentiated — so many kinds of salt, so many names for mercury, so many styles and shapes of instruments.

The radical idiosyncrasy of, and yet deep concordance among, method, problem, and subjectivity also account for why depth psychology finds alchemy so useful a background for the work in its laboratories: the consulting rooms where *nigredo* conditions are all too familiar.

We may read backwards this conformity among worker, that worked on, and way of working backwards; such a reading may offer psychological insights that cannot be gained from a Cartesian-Newtonian science which separates worker from the work. From alchemy, we learn that if you as a worker in any field on any project — from research to marriage, from business to painting — become exhausted, dried out, stuck, depressed, and confused, then you have indications of a *nigredo* phase, and the material you are encountering is itself dark and obstinate. This "depression" signifies a failure neither of your personality nor of your method. In fact, the very difficulties in your method and the darkness of your fantasies indicate that you are in the right place and doing the right thing just because of the darkness.

The optimistic and more Christianized readings of alchemical texts give the *nigredo* mainly an early place in the work, emphasizing progress away from it to better conditions, when blackness will be overcome and a new day of the *albedo* will resurrect from obfuscation and despair. Christianized readings seem unable to avoid salvationalism (Edinger 1985).

This, however, is only one possible reading. The texts make very clear that the *nigredo* is not identical with the *materia prima*, a much larger basket of conditions. The *nigredo* is not the beginning, but an accomplished stage. Black is, in fact, an achievement! It is a condition of something having been worked upon, as charcoal is the result of fire acting on a naive and natural condition of wood, as black feces are the result of digested blood, as blackened fungus is the result of putrefaction and decay. Although depression, fixations, obsessions, and a general blackening of mood and vision may first bring a person to therapy, these conditions indicate that the soul is already engaged in its opus. The psychological initiation began before therapy's first hour. Jung says of the *nigredo*, "the *magnum opus* begins at this point" (1963, 14: paragraph 708).

Black Intentions

What does black intend to achieve? Why is it an accomplishment? Let me briefly list what blackening performs, without using the mystical language of John of the Cross, Simone Weil, and other proponents of religious darkness.

First, as non-color, black extinguishes the perceptual colored world. Second, the blackening negates the "light," whether that be the light of knowledge, the attachment to color consciousness as far-seeing prediction, or the feeling that phenomena can be understood. Black dissolves meaning and the hope for meaning. We are thus benighted. Third, the two processes most relevant for producing blackness — putrefaction and mortification — break down the inner cohesion of any fixed state. Putrefaction, by decomposition or falling apart; mortification, by grinding down — as seeds in a mortar are refined into ever thinner and smaller particles. Newton himself wrote: "For the production of *black*, the Corpuscles must be less than any of those which exhibit Colours" (Dobbs 1975, 224).

This "subtle dissolver," when mixed into other hues, brings about their darkening and deepening, or in alchemical psychology's language — their suffering. Black steers all varieties of brightness into the shade. Is corruption, then, black's intention?

An answer depends on what is meant by "shade." Surely, this intention is not merely the sullying of innocence, the staining of the only natural — that necessary preliminary to all alchemical thinking. Hence, we are not dealing merely with the corruption of natural innocence. The "shade" that black afflicts pertains to the deeper and invisible realm of shades, the Kingdom of Hades, which is the ultimate "subtle dissolver" of the luminous world.

The thickness and solidity of the materials he worked with, Newton said, became more attenuated by fire and by putrefaction, "the more subtle dissolver." Black matter was the least formed and the most susceptible to dissolution — or in our language, chaos.

We can begin to see — through a glass darkly — why the color black is condemned to be a "non-color." It carries the meanings of the random and the formless. Like a black hole, it sucks into it and makes vanish the fundamental security structures of Western consciousness.

By absenting color, black prevents phenomena from presenting their virtues. Black's deconstruction of any positivity — experienced as doubt, negative thinking, suspicion, undoing, valuelessness — explains why the *nigredo* is necessary to every paradigm shift.

Black breaks the paradigm; it dissolves whatever we rely upon as real and dear. Its negative force deprives consciousness of its dependable and comforting notions of goodness. If knowledge be the good, then black confuses it with clouds of unknowing; if life be the good, then black stands for death; if moral virtues be the good, then black means evil. If nature is conceived as a many-colored splendor, then black signifies the entire *opus contra naturam*, translating the great phenomenal world into the inked abstractions of letters, numbers, and lines, replacing the palpable and visual given with the data of marks and traces. By deconstructing presence into absence, the *nigredo* makes possible psychological change.

Therefore, each moment of blackening is a harbinger of alteration, of invisible discovery, and of dissolution of attachments to whatever has been taken as truth and reality, solid fact, or dogmatic virtue. It darkens and sophisticates the eye so that it can see through. Thus, black often becomes the color of dress for the underworld, urban sophisticates, and the old who have seen a lot.

Because black breaks the comforting paradigms, it is the color preferred by the spiritually driven and politically pressuring reformers and "outsiders" — adolescents, rebels, pirates, ladies of the night, cultists, bikers, satanists, puritans, anarchists, hitmen, priests — all the "non-conformists" who then become trapped by their own identification with black, confusing a stage of being with a state of being.

Though alchemical maxims say the work must resemble a "raven's head" in its blackness and that this raven is "the principle of the art," these sayings identify the depth of black's radicality. They do not intend radical identity or identification with black. Black is itself not a paradigm, but a paradigm breaker. That is why it is placed as a phase within a process of colors, and why it appears again and again, in life and in work, in order to deconstruct *(solve et coagula)* what has become an identity. Those who wear the black shirt and the black robe, the black hood, and black undergarments as signs of radical identity become thereby neither anarchists, outsiders, nor reformers, but fundamentalists. Hence, the rigid severity and monotheistic literalism of revolutionaries.

Alchemical psychology teaches us to read as accomplishments the fruitlessly bitter and dry periods, the melancholies that seem never to end, the wounds that do not heal to the *status quo ante,* the grinding sadistic mortifications of shame, and the putrefactions of love and friendships. These are beginnings because they are endings, dissolutions, deconstructions. But they are not the beginning, as a one-time-only occurrence. Such would be a literal reading of the alchemical process, which is not a unidirectional model, progressing in time. It is an *iteratio;* black repeats in order for the deconstruction to continue, as shown for instance by Figure Nine of Jung's commentary on the alchemical *Rosarium* (1954, 16: 285). The soul returns, the king and queen are joined —

yet out of the ground emerge the dark birds.

I do not wish to leave you in this black state, as if I were a Savanarola preacher, a transalpine Lutheran, or a Biblical Jeremiah. I want neither to condemn you to blackness nor to relieve you from it by promising the return of the colored world which alchemical psychology presents in gorgeous images.

Blacker than Black

I am moved by another intention: to warn. And warning, too, belongs to the *nigredo,* for it speaks with the voice of the raven, foretelling dire happenings that may result from the seduction of black. Remember how nineteenth-century colonials feared going black; how Joseph Conrad perceived a madness and a horror in the heart of darkness; how the black plague, the black knight, the black shirt, and the black inquisitor haunt historical Europe; and how the scariest images of childhood — from chimney sweep, magician, black widow, the Rotweiler and the Doberman, to skeletons in the *danse macabre* and the grim reaper himself — stalk the halls of fantasy — all in black. To socialize these fears into race relations does not get at the archetypal imagination of these fears.

Let us be clear: Negro is not *nigredo,* although a figure in a dream called "black," as any dream phenomenon so named, may usher in, and represent, the blackening. But especially in a racist society, we must keep very distinct the epithets that arbitrarily color human beings on the one hand, and, on the other, cosmic forces that shape the soul apart from human beings. What civilized society fears is black magic: the magical pull of black attraction, the soul's desire to descend into darkness, like Persephone unto Hades.[3] We fear what we most desire and desire what we most fear.

The essence of this fear lies in the black radix itself: that it is implacable, indelible, permanent, a crucial component of the *aqua permanens* — that sense of psychic reality underlining and underlying all other realities, like an awareness of death.

Thus, the tragic paradox of black. It sticks like tar to its own self-same negativity. As it curses other colors by darkening their brightness, it curses itself as well, by making itself "blacker than black," beyond the touch of Mercurius duplex.

In other words, the color required for change deprives itself of change, tending to become ever more literal, reductive, and severe. Of all alchemical colors, black is the most densely inflexible and, therefore, the most oppressive and dangerously literal state of soul. Hence, clinicians fear that *nigredo* conditions of depression will lead to literal suicide, revengeful anger to violence, and hatred to domestic cruelty. Hence, too, reductive moves and "shadow" work in therapy feel so concrete and confining.

Of course, as painters know, there are many saturations of black. Part of the painter's *opus* is the differentiation of blacks — blacks that recede and absorb, those that dampen and soften, those that etch and sharpen, and others that shine almost with effulgence — a *sol niger*. Nonetheless, the alchemical maxim "blacker than black" states an ultimate radicality beyond all different shades and varieties. What is blacker than black is the archetypal essence of darkness itself, at times named by alchemy as night, satan, sin, raven, chaos, *tenebrositas*, black dog, and death.

Since Mercurius is hidden and the *albedo* an unpredictable grace, what can "cure" the *nigredo*? What can release the soul from its sombre identification? Decapitation. The black spirit is to be beheaded, an act which, according to Jung (1963, 14: paragraph 730), separates understanding from its identification with suffering. Because, "in the *nigredo* the brain turns black" (Jung 1963, 14: paragraph 733), decapitation "emancipates the *cogitatio.*" Blackness remains, but the distinction between head and body creates a two, where one is imprisoned in singleness. The mind may begin to recognize what the body only feels. Of course, this alchemical "body" is not merely the physical flesh and its symptoms, but all imaginal perspectives that are trapped in habitual concretisms.

Perhaps one of those habitual concretisms is the Newtonian convention — the exclusion of black from the spectrum. Perhaps, the fault is not Newton's at all, but results from black's cursed literalism — its desire to be outside this world, in the underworld, in the dark kingdom of death. Perhaps, black cannot lift the curse from off its own head, and it is thus our job, each of ours, to decapitate the *nigredo*, to emancipate our minds in a post-Newtonian manner, so that we never lose the dark eye and never ignore the soul's desire for shades and sorrow. Maybe, this freeing of the mind not only to see black, but also to see by means of black, would bear as well upon the chaos and tragedy of what are called "race relations," and which are reflections in the human sphere of alchemical processes, whose intentions may be the reanimating of the darkness of matter and the recognition of the sublime beauty of Hades.

By continuing to regard black as a non-color and excluding it from the bright beauty of the Newtonian spectrum, our cosmology remains unable to find a place for the *nigredo* except as "shadow" phenomena such as crime, cruelty, racism, toxicity, and the mental disorder of depression. Also, our sciences, by locating *nigredo* phenomena only in subjectivity as human moods and human failures, continue a delusional method that separates the work from the worker, and from the ecological world worked on.

Worse is the danger that our Western epistemology loses its ability to correct its own bright blindnesses by making radical paradigm shifts. The conversion of black from non-color to color is, therefore, not merely an issue of societal reform regarding the inclusion of darker peoples and darker shades of existence. The inclusion of black among the colors becomes a way Western consciousness might break the naive fundamentalism of its hopefully colored illusions.

Notes

[1] Parts of this paper were first read at the inaugural evening of the "Colors of Life" Conference and Festival in Torino, Italy, August 1995.

[2] See Hillman (1986) for a fuller treatment of the racial implications of color terms.

[3] See Hillman (1979) for a fuller treatment of the Hades realm.

Bibliography

Berlin, Brent and Paul Kay. 1969. *Basic Color Terms: Their Universality and Evolution.* Berkeley: University of California Press.

Boyer, Carl B. 1987. *The Rainbow, From Myth to Mathematics.* Princeton: Princeton University Press.

Dobbs, B.J.T. 1975. *The Foundations of Newton's Alchemy.* Cambridge: Cambridge University Press.

Durand, Gilbert. 1963. *Les structures anthropologiques de l'imaginaire.* Paris: Presses Universitaires.

Edinger, Edward F. 1985. *Anatomy of the Psyche: Alchemical Symbolism in Psychotherapy.* LaSalle, Illinois: Open Court.

Hillman, James. 1979. *The Dream and the Underworld.* New York: Harper / Collins.

——. 1986. "Notes on White Supremacy." *Spring.* Dallas: Spring Publications.

Jung, C.G. 1954. *The Practice of Psychotherapy. Collected Works* 16. Princeton, New Jersey: Pantheon Books.

——. 1963. *Mysterium Coniunctionis. Collected Works* 14. Princeton, New Jersey: Pantheon Books.

Turner, Victor. 1967. *The Forest of Symbols.* Ithaca: Cornell University Press.

Chapter 3

Childhood Seduction: Material and Immaterial Facts

Paul K. Kugler

Introduction

The dramatic appearance in recent years of childhood seduction as a clinical condition and social problem raises fundamental questions for depth psychology. It has been one hundred years since the inception of psychoanalysis, and the same clinical phenomenon that first preoccupied Freud and Jung has now returned to center stage in professional debates. In the past century, many refinements have been accomplished in psychological theory, analytic technique, and clinical practice, but we still find ourselves struggling over the nature and status of psychic images. The exact relation among psychic images, personal history, and psychopathology remains shrouded in mystery. No certitude exists in the profession as to what the patient's psychic image of childhood seduction refers. One theory reduces the image to a traumatic event in early childhood. Another theory refers it to an unconscious wish. Yet another approaches the image of seduction as an attempt at integration of unconscious contents directed by the Self. And still other theories reduce the image to frame violations, transference and counter-transference dynamics, or archetypal constellations. And finally, the more eclectic approaches view the image from various combinations of the above perspectives.

The current debate over how to approach therapeutically the role of childhood seduction in personality formation stretches between two extremes. On one side, we find those therapists specializing in multiple personality disorder and approaching the patient's psychic images from the perspective of traumatic early childhood events that have become dissociated from the patient's more stable conscious identity. These split-off parts of the psyche begin to live a relatively autonomous existence in the personality, creating conditions ranging from dissociative disorder to multiple personality disorder. On the other side of the controversy, we find the patient's psychic images being approached as a result of False Memory Syndrome. From this perspective, the fragmentary memories of childhood seduction and abuse are approached as the patient's desire to separate from the family to which she/he is unconsciously tied. The patient is viewed as having intense guilt about separating from the family and unconsciously blaming the parents' excessive love for their inability to stand alone. This dependency dates back to early childhood and has left the person with a feeling of hostile dependency on the parents, which, in adult life, manifests in the form of destructive fantasies of child-hood seduction and/or abuse. Through the verbalization of these fantasies, separation from the family is achieved.

This debate over how, therapeutically, to interpret psychic images strikes at the very heart of depth psychology and cannot be simply turned into a question of what is "fact" and what is "fantasy"? The difficulty with this issue and what makes it so psychologically poignant is that a certain "truth" subtly resides on both sides of the debate. Each side presents cogent theoretical arguments and graphic clinical examples to defend its position. There are cases where the patient has been physically seduced and abused as a child and later develops a dissociative disorder to cope with this reality. Also, there are cases where the patient was never touched physically, but as a child was emotionally abused, molested through inappropriate looking, and exposed to a family dynamic with a lack of psychic boundaries. And there are also cases where the adult patient, out of his/her own confusion and suffering, tells of seduction and abuse that did not literally happen, but through these images, the patient is able to psychi-cally integrate the darker side of the family that never was allowed to be experienced literally as a child.

Where does the truth lie in these cases? Does it reside in the material or the immaterial facts? It, instead, resides in a subtle appreciation of both. Each patient's psychic images must be believed by the therapist to contain a certain truth about the real-ity of their personality and their developmental history. The diffi-culty will set in when the therapist attempts to make claims about reality and truth that extend beyond the possibilities of the analytic relationship. Criminal courts with extensive means of research at their disposal often find it impossible to sort out the "facts" in these cases. How, then, can we expect the therapist in a closed therapeutic vessel to do what social workers, detectives, lawyers, and polygraphs fail to do? And yet, at times, certain therapists do claim to know what is "real." I want to suggest that often this knowledge of "the real" has been unconsciously imported into the therapeutic encounter through the implicit assumptions contained in the therapist's personal theory of neurosis. And rarely are the therapist's theoretical assumptions subjected to the same careful analysis as the patient's clinical material.

This study will focus on an analysis of the implicit assumptions various psychoanalytic theories import into the therapeutic relationship to explain the aetiological significance of memory-images and fantasies of childhood sexual abuse. My intention is neither to offer a solution to the problem of child sexual abuse nor to provide a theory of it, nor even to explain how to treat it therapeutically in children or in later life. Rather, I would like to develop a greater appreciation of how the therapist's theory of neurosis plays a significant role in determining what is experienced as real and true in the clinical encounter by the patient. Let us turn to the history of childhood seduction in depth psychology and explore some of the underlying psychotherapeutic assumptions held by the founders of psychoanalysis.

Freud's Seduction Theory

The first significant aetiological explanation of neurosis in depth psychology was Freud's seduction theory. To understand the deeper issues motivating Freud's theory, we must locate the event historically. The dominant theory of neurosis in 1896 claimed "heredity," namely, congenital degeneration with the presence of cerebral lesions, to be the primary cause of hysterical symptoms. According to the heredity theory, the parents were passive transmitters of the disease to the child through genetics. Against this background, Freud developed his new seduction theory, according to which the parents were now conceived as actively creating hysterical symptoms in the child through seductive actions.

Shifting the cause of the neurosis from the forefathers to the "actual" fathers, Freud wrote: "The foundation for a neurosis would accordingly always be laid in childhood by an adult" (1962a, 208-09).

Persons suffering from neurosis, according to the new theory, had been sexually abused as children by their parents, older siblings, or parental substitutes. To account for the transmission of hysteria from generation to generation, Freud formulated the phylogenetic dictum, "heredity is seduction by the father" (1954, 180). No longer were the parents viewed as passively transmitting hysteria to their children through genetics. Now, the parental figure was viewed as actively creating hysteria in the child through seductive behavior.

By the spring of 1896, Freud had treated eighteen analytic cases, all of which seemed to confirm his new hypothesis. He developed a therapeutic method based upon this hypothesis, which causally linked the current neurotic symptoms, through a chain of verbal associations, to a past sexual trauma. The seduction theory clearly implicated child sexual abuse, in both its gross and its subtle forms, as being pathogenic and "more" fundamental in neurotic symptom formation than heredity.

So aware was Freud of his challenge to the heredity theory that in February of 1896 he sent off for publication two papers dealing with the dispute over the origin of hysteria. One paper, "Heredity and the Aetiology of the Neuroses" (Freud 1962b, 142-56), written for a French publication, criticized the disciples of Charcot, his former teacher, for holding to heredity as the primary aetiology of neurosis; the second paper, "Further Remarks on the Neuropsychoses of Defence" (Freud 1962c, 159-85), written for German physicians, presented a similar critique.

Freud's theoretical shift away from heredity and the neuropathological model had already begun in 1893 with his short book entitled *On Aphasia*. There, Freud shows that even where there is an organic lesion, the explanation of the aphasic phenomenon of verbal dissociation — the splitting of one idea off from another — must be understood independently of the anatomical location of the lesion. This theoretical shift from conceiving verbal pathology as a result of a brain lesion to conceiving it as a result of the splitting of an idea off from consciousness opened the way to a completely new understanding of hysteria for Freud. Neurotic symptoms result from a splitting, which occurs in the mind, not in the cerebral cortex. In hysteria, the mind develops a "lesion" when a specific idea is cut off from consciousness. If an idea is split off, dissociated from the conscious mind as in hysteria, then what causes the splitting? What is the origin of the mental lesion?

Freud's answer to this question was ingeniously simple and economical: a mental lesion is created by a psychic "trauma," the trauma of childhood seduction. Sexually traumatic events in childhood give rise to mental lesions — split-off ideas not verbally expressed and remaining outside the realm of consciousness. Later in life, these split-off parts of the mind find expression through neurotic or psychotic symptoms.

Freud's new explanation for the origin of mental lesions — hysterical symptoms — deliteralizes an older, neuropathological idea. Traditional neurology held that a physical trauma to the head could result in a cerebral lesion. Freud's new theory suggested that a sexual trauma to the child's mind could result in a psychic lesion.

The Deliteralization of Seduction

The origin of psychoanalysis can be read as a deliteralizing of the traditional medical concepts of brain, lesion, and trauma. Freud's progressive deliteralization of medical concepts took a dramatic shift on 21 September 1897, when in a published and much-studied letter, Freud wrote Fliess to confide his discovery that some of the stories of childhood seduction by the father, as told by his patients, were fantasies. This discovery called into question the very foundation of his seduction theory. Perhaps, no aspect in the history of psychoanalysis has been more analyzed, exalted, and distorted than this letter of 21 September 1897. While many praise it as the origin of psychoanalysis and others condemn it as dismissing the stories of seduction as mere fantasies, it seems few have actually read Freud's original letter. The ideas contained in this letter have been so distorted through the selective editing of Alice Miller, Jeffery Masson, Milton Klein, and others who are trying to resurrect the seduction theory that to help clarify the reasons for Freud's decision, we need to read the entire section of the letter dealing with his seduction theory, or the "neurotica" as he called it.

21 September 1897
My dear Wilhelm,

Here I am again, arrived yesterday morning, refreshed, cheerful, impoverished, at present without work, and, having settled in again, I am writing to you first.

And now I want to confide in you immediately the great secret of something that in the past few months has gradually dawned on me. I no longer believe in my NEUROTICA. This is probably not intelligible without an explanation; after all, you yourself found what I was able to tell you credible. So I will begin historically and tell you from where the reasons for rejecting it came. The first group of factors were the continual disappointment in my attempts to bring my analyses to a real conclusion; the running away of people who for a time had seemed my most favourably inclined patients, the lack of the complete success on which I had counted, and the possibility of explaining to myself the partial successes in other, familiar, ways. Then there was the astonishing thing that in every case the father, not excluding my own, had to be accused of being perverse, and the unexpected realization of the frequency of hysteria, with precisely the same conditions prevailing in each case, whereas surely such widespread perversions against children are not very probable. (The [incidence] of perversion would have to be immeasurably more frequent than the [resulting] hysteria because the illness, after all, occurs only where there has been an accumulation of events and there is a contributory factor that weakens the defense.) Then, third, the certain insight that there is no "indication of reality" in the unconscious, so that one cannot distinguish between truth and fiction that has been cathected with affect. (This leaves open the possible explanation that sexual phantasy regularly makes use of the theme of the parents.) Fourthly, there was the consideration that even in the most deep-reaching psychoses the unconscious memory does not break through, so that the secret of infantile experiences is not revealed even in the most confused states of delirium. When one thus sees that the unconscious never overcomes the resistance of the conscious, the expectation diminishes that in treatment the reverse process will take place to the extent that the unconscious is completely tamed by consciousness.

So far was I influenced by these considerations that I was ready to abandon two things — the complete solution of a neurosis and sure reliance on its aetiology in infancy. Now I do not know where I am, as I have not succeeded in gaining a theoretical understanding of repression and its interplay of forces. It once again seems arguable that only later experiences give the impetus to phantasies which throw back to childhood; and with this, the factor of an hereditary disposition regains a sphere of influence from which I had made it my business to oust it — in the interest of fully explaining neurosis.

Were I depressed, jaded, unclear in my mind, such doubts might be taken as signs of weakness. But as I am in just the opposite state, I must acknowledge them to be the result of honest and effective intellectual labour, and I am proud that after penetrating so far I am still capable of such criticism. Can these doubts be only an episode on the way to further knowledge?
(This translation is a composite of James Strachey and Jeffrey Massons' earlier translations, and of my own.)

In the letter, Freud gives four sets of reasons for giving up his seduction theory. The first set has to do with his most favorable patients leaving therapy without the analytic treatment producing the therapeutic success he had anticipated. Freud had encountered unexplainable transference and counter-transference reactions. The second set of reasons focuses on his discovery that, in every case, the patient's current problem was blamed on perverse acts by the father and that the incidence of perversion would have to be much greater than the incidence of hysteria to account for an actual traumatic aetiology. Third, and perhaps most important, Freud realizes that there is no "indication of reality" in the unconscious.

The phrase, "indication of reality," is surrounded by quotation marks in order to remind Fliess of his previous use of the phrase in the "Project for a Scientific Psychology." Two years earlier, in 1895, Freud had used the phrase in the "Project" in the context of a discussion of his second "biological rule of attention." Freud had constructed the rule to account for how the ego differentiates real perceptions from wishes or apperceptions. The actual rule in the "Project" reads: "The indications of discharge or the indications of quality are also primarily indications of `reality,' and are intended to serve the purpose of distinguishing the cathexes of real percep- tions from the cathexes of wishes" (Freud 1954, 429). Freud believed ego-consciousness was capable of qualitatively differenti- ating real perceptions from wishes and desires based upon the quality of the neurological discharge or cathexes. Whether or not this is neurologically accurate, it was a part of Freud's belief system at the time.

Suddenly in the fall of 1897, Freud found himself again confronted with the problem of differentiating outer perceptions from inner fantasies and wishes. This time, however, he was deal- ing not with the ego and its problem of attention, but rather with the unconscious and memory-images. His conclusion this time was that in the unconscious, there is "no" "indication of reality." This realization led Freud to write in his letter of 21 September: "it is impossible to distinguish between truth and emotionally- charged fiction." If this is the case, Freud reasoned, then emotion- ally-charged inner sexual desires can regularly make use of memory-images of the outer parents.

The final reason Freud presents for giving up his seduction theory and a therapy based on bringing to consciousness the person's "outer" childhood history is the realization that even in the most acute psychoses and states of delirium, all the memories of outer infantile experiences do not surface. Therefore, the goal of therapy cannot be to recover completely all of one's childhood memories.

On the basis of these four considerations, Freud expanded — not abandoned, as has been charged — his previous aetiology of neurosis, so as to include the role of fantasy in symptom-forma- tion. On 27 April 1898, Freud wrote to Fliess: "Initially I defined the aetiology too narrowly; the share of fantasy in it is far greater than I had thought in the beginning" (1954, 252).

The Expanded Aetiology

In expanding his aetiology, Freud did not abandon the awareness that actual, historical seductions occur, nor did he abandon the idea of seduction as a psychic reality. Rather, he discovered that fantasies of seduction can appear in memory, even when no physical seduction has taken place. The child can be seduced psychologically by the desire of the external other, or the internal other, even when no physical acts have taken place. The significance of this discovery can, and has been, distorted, but it cannot be overemphasized. For Freud had discovered that memory records not only perceptions, but also wishes and apperceptions. Memory is a confabulated record of the events occurring in the exterior environment, along with those events occurring in the interior environment. Furthermore, in the unconscious there is no "indication of reality"; therefore, it is impossible to distinguish between history and desire.

Freud's new theory posited the existence of a psychic life of fantasy, in large part unconscious, coexisting in the personality along with memories of actual historical events. These fantasy-images Freud derived ontogenetically from the unfolding of instinctual drives and apperceived bodily feelings. These erotic and aggressively toned fantasy images comingle with historical memory images in the Id, and their dynamic interrelation with the parental imagos, Freud termed the Oedipus complex. His new theory viewed the Oedipus complex and the vicissitudes of Id psychology as the primary, but not the only, motivating forces structuring the personality. The role of the outer environment was never denied by Freud. But the problem for Freud, and later for Jung, was how to explain the fact that many adults suffer childhood seduction, yet only certain individuals subsequently develop psychic disturbances. And, furthermore, why is it that certain adults who have never been sexually molested as children, but who later fantasize about being molested, also develop these same psychic disorders. As to whether the actual seduction or the fantasized seduction has a greater pathogenic effect, Freud wrote: "We have not succeeded in pointing to any difference in the consequences, whether phantasy or reality has the greater share."

Freud never denied the reality of his patients' memories of actual childhood traumas, as some writers have suggested. Rather, he recognized that the memories of actual childhood are continually being confabulated with unconscious fantasies. Moreover, in the context of the closed analytic vessel, it is almost impossible to distinguish which aspects of unconscious images refer to outer objective perceptions and which refer to inner desires and fantasies.

Jung's Aetiology

Jung wrote an early essay on the function of childhood memories in the aetiology of neurosis which is particularly significant to our discussion. The essay, entitled "The Theory of Psychoanalysis," consists of seven lectures given in September 1912 at Fordham University Medical School. It is nearly 150 pages in length, and some of the more relevant subsections are entitled: "The Theory of Sexual Trauma in Childhood," "The Predisposition for the Trauma," "The Sexual Element in the Trauma," "Infantile Sexual Fantasy," "Unconscious Fantasy Systems," "The Oedipus Complex," "The Aetiology of Neurosis," and "The Aetiological Significance of the Actual Present." Discussing the aetiological significance of historical traumata and its relation to imaginary traumata, Jung writes:

> We are thus obliged to assume that many traumata in early infancy are of a purely fantastic nature, mere fantasies in fact, while others do have objective reality. With this discovery, somewhat bewildering at first sight, the aetiological significance of the sexual trauma in childhood falls to the ground, as it now appears totally irrelevant whether the trauma really occurred or not. Experience shows us that fantasies can be just as traumatic in their effects as real traumata.... We know very well that there are a great many more people who experience traumata in childhood or adult life without getting a neurosis. Therefore the trauma, other things being equal, has no absolute aetiological significance and will pass off without having any lasting effect. From this simple reflection it is perfectly clear that the individual must meet the trauma with a quite definite inner predisposition in order to make it really effective. This inner predisposition is not to be understood as that obscure, hereditary disposition of which we know so little, but as a psychological development which reaches its

climax, and becomes manifest, at the traumatic moment (Jung 1961, 4: paragraphs 216-17).

We must remember that at the time this was written, the prevailing aetiologies located the determining factors, either internally, in the form of hereditary predisposition, or environmentally, in the form of actual childhood traumata. Both Freud and Jung were working to formulate a new aetiological vision locating the determining factors midway between the environment and the personal psychology of the patient. In discussing the prevailing explanations and his new epigenetic aetiology, Jung writes:

> It is the fashion nowadays to regard all mental abnormalities not of exogenous origin as consequences of hereditary degeneration, and not as essentially conditioned by *the psychology of the patient and his environment* [my emphasis]. But this is an extreme view which fails to do justice to the facts. We know very well how to find the middle course in dealing with the aetiology of tuberculosis. There are undoubtedly cases of tuberculosis where the germ of the disease proliferates from early childhood in soil predisposed by heredity, so that even under the most favourable conditions the patient cannot escape his fate. But there are also cases where there is no hereditary taint and no predisposition, and yet a fatal infection occurs. This is equally true of the neuroses, where things will not be radically different from what they are in general pathology. An extreme theory about predisposition will be just as wrong as an extreme theory about environment (Jung 1961, 4: paragraph 209).

Jung's opts for an epigenetic aetiology midway between Aristotle's empiricism and Plato's nativism. This hypothesis means the pathogenic experience occurring in the outer environment, for example, a childhood seduction, is supplemented by an inner psychological factor. A combination of perception and apperception, outer history and inner emotional response, determines the pathogenesis.

The Confluence of History and Emotion

Material history and emotional reactions come together in memory. To retrieve the historical events of childhood, the analyst must rely on the patient's memory of what happened. In the course of analysis, memories in various forms are continually being analyzed. These memory-images may be of the previous analytic session, the events of the past week, a recent dream, a story about the patient's parents, or an event from childhood. Common to all these memories is that they are images of some other event. And these images arise from a conjunction of outer environmental influences, plus the specific reactions of the individual. The mental image, therefore, reflects any actual historical event with very considerable qualification. The composite memory-image, the imago as Jung referred to it, is itself a distinct psychological entity. The imago exists independently of the historical referent, even if based in part on perception.

Just here, the difficulty problem arises. As long as the image is identified with the actual behavior of the object in the outer world, for example, the erotically excited father-imago identified with the actual father, the presence of the image as a distinct psychological entity within the patient's personality will remain unconscious. The conscious mind cannot recognize the relative autonomy of composite images because the images are projected back onto the object world and confused with the object's own autonomy. Psychic reality is fused with physical reality; the finger pointing at the moon is confused with the moon itself; the world of images is identified with the world of material history. In short: the image is contaminated by the object. In contemporary painting, the distinction between object and imago has been ingeniously portrayed by Rene Magritte. His painting of a green meerschaum pipe has for its title (in English translation): "This is not a pipe."

The realization of the psychological importance in analysis of differentiating the object from its imago led Jung no longer only to speak of historical childhood and historical parents, but also to employ the term "imago." Jung discusses the reason for this decision in the following section from his Fordham University lectures:

> Among the things that were of the upmost significance at the infantile period the most influential are the personalities of the parents. Even when the parents have long been dead and lost, or should have lost, all significance, the situation of the patient having perhaps completely changed since then, they

are still somehow present and as important as if they were
still alive. The patient's love, admiration, resistance, hatred,
and rebelliousness still cling to their effigies, transfigured by
affection or distorted by envy, and often bearing little resemblance to the erstwhile reality. It was this fact that compelled
me to speak no longer of "father" and "mother" but to employ
instead the term "imago," because these fantasies are not
concerned any more with real father and mother but with
subjective and often very much distorted images of them
which lead a shadowy but nonetheless potent existence in the
patient's mind (Jung 1961, 4: paragraph 305).

The imago bears traces of both external and internal history.
Impressions of the external world entering via the perceptual
systems are affected by the particular emotional reactions of the
perceiver. The person's love, admiration, resistance, hatred, rebelliousness, and envy transfigure the perceptual contents, producing
an imago. The perceiver's emotional reactions are recorded in
memory through the transfigurations of the actual perceptual
contents.

In 1916, Jung characterized the imago as an autonomous
psychic presence within the personality, even if derived from a
conjunction of outer perceptions and inner emotional reactions. In
"The Relation Between the Ego and the Unconscious," Jung
writes:

> The simple soul is of course unaware of the fact that his near-
> est relations who exercise immediate influence over him,
> create in him an image which is only partly a replica of them-
> selves, while its other part is compounded of elements derived
> from himself. The imago is built up of parental influences plus
> the specific reactions of the child; it is therefore an image that
> reflects the object with very considerable qualifications.... The
> image is unconsciously projected, and when the parents die,
> the projected image goes on working as though it were a spirit
> existing on its own. The primitive then speaks of parental
> spirits who return by night ("revenants"), while the modern
> man calls it a father or mother complex. (1961, 7: paragraph
> 294).

In *Symbols of Transformations,* Jung again emphasizes the
crucial differentiation between the physical parents and the
parental imagos:

Interpretation in terms of the parents is, however, simply a matter of speaking. In reality the whole drama takes place in the individual's own psyche, where the "parents" are not the parents at all but only their imagos; they are representations which have arisen from the conjunction of parental peculiarities with the individual disposition of the child (1961, 5: paragraph 505).

The "imago" is the merging place of perception and apperception. And because of this merging, no one can ever fully distinguish between remembered history and imagined fantasy. When confronted with the realization that from the perspective of the imago there can never be complete separation of history and fantasy, perception from apperception, and that in many instances we can not determine whether or not there was actual physical abuse, then also, we must accept that whenever abuse is reported by patients, "abuse" is actually occurring. The therapist must believe the patient's story, regardless of whether it is based on material or immaterial facts. Hearing the story as historical remembering does not necessarily make it more "real" — except in those cases where the person's *Weltanschauung* requircs history to authenticate reality. And we must keep in mind that certain patients or therapists may need to experience an image in the form of a historical memory in order for that image to be felt as a real happening.

The problem is not whether or not the patient suffers from childhood seduction or abuse. Of course the patient does, and such abuse exists simply because the patient says it exists. The abuse exists as a psychic fact. The real problem is in how the treating therapist approaches the patient's image. Furthermore, how the analyst therapeutically enters the image will reveal the analyst's own unconscious working definition of reality and theory of neurosis.

If the therapist derives psychic reality from the physical and the historical, then physical, historical seduction will be considered the preponderant aetiological factor. If, however, the therapist defines psychic reality more in terms of wishes, desires, and archetypal images, then these factors will be considered more aetiologically significant. And, finally, if the therapist works from the definition of reality that both the environment and the individual emotional responses of the person are equally real, then a combination of these factors will determine the aetiology.

From this perspective, the problematics of abuse become paradigmatic for understanding the therapist's sense of psychic reality. To stay with the imago, that merging place of perception and apperception, historical autobiography and emotionally charged fiction, keeps the analyst and patient always in psychic reality and aware of the primacy in analysis of this reality over all other realities.

Jung's theory of interpretation, based upon an objective and a subjective level, provides a therapeutic method for working with this interaction between history and fantasy. The objective level refers the imago to the outer historical event through the process of free association. The subjective level, on the other hand, refers the same psychic image to inner events. The therapeutic movement between objective and subjective levels encourages the individual to confront both the reality of the environment and outer history, as well as the reality of subjective imaginings and emotional responses.

The Psychology of Rumour

Between 1910 and 1911 Jung again dealt with the problem of childhood sexuality and the intermingling of objective and subjective history. This time, he approached the problem from the perspective of social dynamics. His essay, "A Contribution to the Psychology of Rumour" (1961), was prompted by a request from the local school authorities for Jung to examine the mental status of a thirteen-year-old high school girl. The student had been expelled from school after her teacher had indirectly heard an ambiguous sexual story involving him, being told by some of his female students. Investigation revealed that Marie, the student who had been referred to Jung, had told three of her classmates of a dream she had had involving her teacher. The dream itself contained nothing scandalous, but as the dream began to circulate from student to student, each new narrator unconsciously supplemented the narrative with elements from his/her own unconscious fantasies and unresolved complexes.

Jung presents eight different versions of the dream collected from various students. The altered dream texts arose from a conjunction of objective elements from the original narrative, intertwined with subjective elements supplied by the new narrators. His analysis of the progressive transformation of the dream text into a rumour disclosed how unconscious sexual complexes lying dormant in each new narrator were "detonated" by the emotionally toned story. The analysis of the various versions of the story revealed that the secondary elaborations supplied by the retellers of the dream actually functioned to interpret the latent content of the dream itself. Jung concludes:

> So far as the interpretation of the dream is concerned, there is nothing for me to add; the children themselves have done all that is necessary, leaving practically nothing over for psychoanalytic interpretation. *The rumour has analyzed and interpreted the dream* (1961, 4: paragraph 125).

Jung's method of analyzing the sexual rumour is particularly instructive. He approaches the events from the perspective of psychological understanding. His analysis is not based upon the constructs of true or false, fact or fantasy, good or bad, guilty or innocent, victim or victimizer. Rather, he starts simply with the reality of the phenomenon itself and attempts to understand its meaning psychologically. His analysis of the transformations of the original dream text into a rumour through the constellation of the dormant complexes in the retellers provides a powerful insight into the evolution of a historical narrative in relation to interpsychic and intrapsychic dynamics.

To understand better today's clinical perspective on the effect of childhood sexual abuse on the adult personality, let us review briefly some of the current research on the long-term impact of child sexual abuse.

The Empirical Perspective

The most comprehensive review of the research to date by is by Angela Browne and David Finkelhor, and it focuses directly on the effect in adult life of childhood sexual abuse. Their research examines three important issues: (1) the incidence of psychopathology in relation to age groups; (2) whether the sexual trauma is the only aetiological factor, or whether there is a premorbid factor already in the child's environment; (3) the general public's "adultocentric" tendency to view abuse from the perspective of "long-term impact."

In regard to the incidence of psychopathology in relation to age groups, the research found that "seventeen percent of four to six-year-olds in the study met the criteria for `significant pathology,'" demonstrating more overall disturbance than a normal population, but less than the norms for other children their age who were in psychiatric care. The highest incidence of psychopathology was found in the seven to thirteen-year-old group, with forty percent scoring in the seriously disturbed range. Intrestingly, few of the adolescent victims were found to exhibit severe psychopathology (Browne and Finkelhor 1986, 68). The research found that sexual abuse from the ages of seven to thirteen produced the highest incidence of clinically significant psychopathology.

Second, concerning the possibility of a premorbid factor brought into the traumatic experience by the child, Browne and Finkelhor note:

> One of the most imposing challenges for researchers is to explore the sources of trauma in sexual abuse. Some of the apparent effects of sexual abuse may be due to premorbid conditions, such as family conflict or emotional neglect, that actually contribute to a vulnerability to abuse and to exacerbating later trauma. Other effects may be due less to the experience itself than to later social reactions to disclosure (1986, 76).

The research confirmed the earlier views of Freud and Jung that the source of the trauma in sexual abuse is a combination of environmental factors plus the specific emotional reaction of the child.

Third, regarding the public's preoccupation with long term effects of childhood abuse, the study's concluding paragraph states:

> Finally, there is an unfortunate tendency in interpreting the effects of sexual abuse (as well as in studies of other childhood trauma) to overemphasize long-term impact as the ultimate criterion. Effects seem to be considered less "serious" if their impact is transient and disappears in the course of development. However, this tendency to assess everything in terms of its long-term effect betrays an "adulto-centric" bias. Adult traumas such as rape are not assessed ultimately in terms of

whether they will have an impact on old age; they are acknowledged to be painful and alarming events, whether their impact lasts one year or ten. Similarly, childhood traumas should not be dismissed because no "long-term effects" can be demonstrated. Child sexual abuse needs to be recognized as a serious problem of childhood, if only for the immediate pain, confusion and upset that can ensue (Browne and Finkelhor 1986, 76).

The research of Browne and Finkelhor presents a descriptive analysis of the impact, the effect, of child sexual abuse, but it does not analyze the cause or aetiology of the syndrome.

Aetiology and the Treatment of Choice

The therapist at the beginning of treatment is often confronted with the question of aetiology. Therapy begins with a differentiation of the patient's presenting symptoms, followed by a consideration of the possible cause or aetiology of the symptoms. Choice of treatment may then derive from how the therapist answers the aetiological question. The answer to the question of aetiology will more often than not be decisively influenced by the therapist's own theoretical commitment — a commitment which implicitly dictates what the major determinants of personality are, and where they are located. If, for example, the therapist views the major determinants of personality to be located in the outer world, then the therapist will look to the patient's actual parents and siblings, bipersonal events, the childhood environment and its history for the aetiology of the patient's symptoms. If, however, the therapist's theoretical commitment views the major determinants of personality to be located in the inner world, then the therapist will look to the patient's Oedipus complex, unconscious drives, typology, complexes, or archetypal images for explanation. The analyst's theoretical commitment has a significant impact on countertransference reactions, as well as on patients' attitudes toward their own symptoms and personal histories. If the analyst's theoretical orientation governs what will be viewed as the pathogenic factors in the patient's personality, then what determines the analyst's choice of theory?

Theory and Types

Jung has suggested that the analyst's choice of theory is partially a result of typology. Extraverts will place greater determining significance on the environmental and objective factors, introverts on the interior and subjective factors. Jung's theory of types attempts to understand psychologically the theoretical differences between Freud and Adler. The theory of types was an ingenious attempt to differentiate the various epistemological constraints imposed by consciousness upon the process of knowing. Interestingly enough, Jung's theory is itself grounded in the introverted perspective, locating the determining factors inside the individual in the form of typological predisposition.

While his analysis focused on those constraints which govern and limit our capacity to know, Jung neglected a second set of constraints which arise from the analyst's implicit ontological commitment. An ontological commitment can be defined simply as the analyst's working definition of reality. A short Persian children's story may help clarify what I mean.

> In Iran a series of children's stories tell about a holy man called Mullah Nasrudin, a sort of Persian counterpart to Uncle Remus. One day Mullah Nasrudin's friends were walking around when suddenly Mullah Nasrudin galloped past them on his horse, apparently looking for something. A short time later, Mullah Nasrudin again galloped past them. This happened several more times, at which point his friends decided to stop and offer to help him in his search. So, when Mullah Nasrudin again came galloping by, his friends stopped him and asked what he was looking for. To this, Mullah Nasrudin replied: "I am looking for my horse."

Our unconscious definition of reality is the horse on which our conscious perspective is mounted. There is, perhaps, no animal that carries more psychic weight, bears more burdens, takes over the reins, and rides away with us more often than our ontology. Our ontological commitment is the fantasy of reality we are unconsciously moved by and which constrains our sense of reality, determining what will be experienced literally and what metaphorically.

The relationship between theory formation and the constraints of being (ontology) and knowing (epistemology), can be imagined as a house built on a lot, with a foundation and many upper stories. The house with its different stories is like the tradition of depth psychology, with its different theoretical narratives. The foundation, a ground floor through which you must pass, and which supports all the various upper stories, is the epistemology. To get at any clinical and empirical data whatsoever, we must pass through an implicit theory of knowledge and, therefore, the limitations of the human mind and its capacity to know.

Jung's theory of psychological types and of the four functions of consciousness is an elaborate differentiation of the various types of epistemological constraints making up the structures of consciousness. While Jung tried to expose the various foundations of knowledge upon which psychological theories are built, he neglected an analysis of the ground upon which the theory itself is built. This ground is called "Being" or "Reality," and the study of its ground rules is ontology. All the various theories of knowledge and all the stories built upon them are grounded on a more fundamental level in a working definition of reality. This unshakeable definition of reality determines the elements in the patient's symptomology and history, which from the therapist's point of view, cannot be seen through, deliteralized. These are the so-called literal realities of the case history which cannot be reduced to some more fundamental reality.

The analyst's aetiological explanation of clinical phenomena is a function of two sets of constraints: knowing and being. The theoretical splits in psychoanalysis have most often occurred on the ontological level, with one faction declaring its ontic structure, its god-term, truer and more real than the others. For example, in the beginning, Freud gave childhood seduction primary ontological status in his theory of neurosis. Later, he shifted the primary ontic structure to internal drives and the Oedipus complex. Subsequent generations of analysts have shifted their "miracle" or first principle, variously from drives, to the mother, to the birth trauma, to the involuntary nervous system, to the child, to the ego and its defense mechanisms, to identity, to types, to archetypes, to the Self, to object-relations, to language, to the bipersonal field, to the gaze, to the soul, and to the imagination. Each new ontological shift has opened up new theoretical visions and provided new narrative truths about personality and its pathology.

Multiple Aetiologies

The aetiology of personality structure and its associated psychopathologies has been dominated by three dramatically different explanatory constructs. Whether one is committed to Aristotle's empiricism, Plato's nativism, or to the current epigenetic variants, the strategy for introducing change therapeutically into the personality is the same: for change to occur, therapy must alter the structure of the constraints that harness the personality. If the constraints are postulated to be in the environment, then therapeutic change will be imagined as changing the environmental schedules. This is the therapeutic strategy adopted by behaviorism. If the constraints are imagined to be located at the physiological level, then therapeutic change will be imagined as changing the interior structures of the person's biochemistry through psychopharmacology. This therapeutic strategy underlies the traditional medical model. And if the constraints are imagined to be located at the interaction between the individual and the environment, then therapeutic change will be imagined as altering this interactional relationship. This strategy is the one adopted by depth psychology. Therapy from this third perspective focuses on changing the relationship between consciousness and the inner environment of unconscious drives and fantasy images, or object-relations with the outer environment. The different schools of thought making up depth psychology differ over which element in the interactional field is viewed as primary and, therefore, which one carries the most aetiological significance.

As an exercise in aetiological explanation, however, all the above approaches suffer from the regress problem. These theories locate the constraints structuring the personality either in the environment, or in the physiology of the person, or in the interaction between consciousness and the interior and/or exterior environments. The regress problem arises when the theorist tries to account for the origin of the constraints themselves. For example, if we take the behaviorist perspective and view the origin of the environmental constraints as a function of a larger organized environment, then that environment must in turn be organized by an even larger context, which is in turn organized by an even larger one, ad infinitum. The behaviorist's aetiology lapses into an environmental regress.

This type of explanation, when applied to the behavioral pattern of childhood sexual abuse, runs something like this: child abuse is caused by the abuser having been sexually abused as a child by another abuser, who had also been abused as a child, all the way back to the primal horde. In other words, if the therapist's definition of reality is such that only the physical environment is imagined to be most real and aetiologically significant, then the therapist will look to the physical environment to find "the real" cause of the disorder.

When this same problem is approached from the interior physiological perspective of the medical model, then the origin of the constraints will be looked for on the biochemical level in the form of an endocrine, hormone, or some other biochemical imbalance. This aetiology will also lapse into the regress problem because the biochemical explanation regresses onto its design principles, genetics, which again regresses the problem back onto previous generations, without ever accounting for the origin of the genetic code.

If the therapist's working definition of reality views the interrelation between consciousness and the person's fantasies as primary, then an aetiology of child abuse will begin with those constraints innate to the interaction between consciousness and psychic images. On the level of Jung's imago, these constraints will be viewed as a function of a more "abstract" set of constraints — the archetype-as-such — which is a function of the psyche's innate capacity to create images or phylogenetically determined patterns of behavior. This aetiology lapses into an archetypal regress, halting only by accounting for the origin of the behavior through an appeal to the innateness hypothesis. On the other interactional-drive level (early Freud), the fantasy-images are reduced to representations of drives, which are then posited as innate first principles. This construct also regresses onto the innateness hypothesis.

Neither is the problem solved by opting for an object-relations or bipersonal approach. In these approaches, the constraints are located either between subjective consciousness and the so-called objective world, or in the intersubjective space. These approaches also lapse into the regress problem for they cannot account for the origin of the structures in the representational world (Winnicott,

Kernberg, Kohut, *et al.*), language (Lacan), or the bipersonal field (Searles, Langs, and Goodheart).

In other words, we simply have no adequate theory for the origin of the complex structures making up the personality and its psychopathology. Most aetiological explanations are merely new descriptions of the clinical phenomenon, not true explanations. And these causal clinical "explanations" often function as self-serving confirmations of the researcher's unconscious ontological and theoretical commitments. A true explanation must account for the emergence of new structural properties or, in this case, syndromes and patterns of behavior. The inability to establish with certainty the aetiology of psychiatric syndromes led the editors of the DSM IV to omit aetiologies from the manual, except where it is indicated in the name of the syndrome itself.

The principle of "causality" is so basic to the idea of aetiology and clinical thinking that rarely is it reflected on, or called into question. Since Newton, the Western mind has taken for granted that causality implies a logical and temporal priority of cause to effect. In the *The Will to Power*, Nietzsche argues that this idea of causal structure is not something given as such, but rather the product of a precise tropological or rhetorical operation, a *"chronologische Umdrehung"* (chronological reversal). Suppose, for example, a patient feels a pain. This causes the patient or doctor to look for a cause. Seeing a traumatic event in the patient's historical past, the doctor posits a link and reverses the perceptual or phenomenal order, pain ... traumatic event, to produce a causal sequence, traumatic event ... pain. Nietzsche concludes:

> The fragment of the outside world of which we become conscious comes after the effect that has been produced on us and is projected *a posteriori* as its "cause." In the phenomenalism of the "inner world," we invent the chronology of cause and effect. The basic fact of "inner experience" is that the cause gets *imagined* [my emphasis] after the effect has occurred (1901, 3: 804).

The causal scheme is produced by a metalepsis, a substitution of cause for effect. Causality is the product of a tropological operation, not an indubitable foundation.

Let us be as specific as possible as to what this simple example implies for clinical aetiologies. It does not lead to the conclusion that causality is invalid and should be avoided as an explanatory principle. On the contrary, causality is an archetypal image essential to the nature of the western psyche. While we cannot escape it, we can see through it, deepening our own consciousness through a psychologizing of the image. Archetypal psychology has shown how every image brings with it the hermeneutics by which it can be interpreted. This also holds true for the image of causality. Notice how the very act of deliteralizing (psychologizing) the image of causality relies itself on the notion of cause: the experience of pain, it is claimed, causes the discovery of the trauma and thus causes the production of a cause. To deliteralize causality, one must operate with the notion of cause and apply it to causation itself. The deliteralization appeals to no higher logical principle or superior reason (for example, the Self), but uses the very image it deliteralizes. The concept of causation is not an error that psychology could, or should, avoid, but is instead an indispensable image based upon a tropological operation.

Conclusion

This essay has focused on an analysis of the implicit assumptions that various psychoanalytic theories import into the therapeutic relationship to explain the aetiological significance of memory-images and fantasies of childhood sexual abuse. This analysis of the analyst's epistemological and ontological assumptions and the influence they have on the aetiological explanation of clinical phenomena may seem far removed from the so-called "real" clinical issues of child sexual abuse. But when responsibly trying to determine whether certain events actually occurred in outer reality and what consequence these events may have on the stuctures of the personality, these questions are simply unavoidable. To gain empirical and clinical knowledge and to attempt to determine what is real, and what is the aetiology of the syndrome, the treating therapist must consciously or, as is more often the case, unconsciously, adopt a theory of knowledge and make an ontological commitment. These unconscious background assumptions significantly affect the development of the therapist's working aetiology of the disorder and the treatment of choice. And, rarely, if ever, are these unconscious background assumptions made part of the clinical record or of the empirical research.

Today, one hundred years after the inception of depth psychology, as our clinical eye once again focuses in on the problem of childhood seduction and its role in symptom formation, we need not only to analyze our patient's personal and family dynamics in relation to these images, but, equally important, to analyze in-depth our own particular clinical theories and the impact their unconscious assumptions have on the interpretation of our patient's clinical material.

Bibliography

Browne, Angela and David Finkelhor. 1986. "Impact of Child Sexual Abuse: A Review of the Research." *Psychological Bulletin* 99, no. 1.

Freud, Sigmund. 1954. *The Origins of Psychoanalysis: Letters to Wilhelm Fliess, Drafts and Notes: 1892-1899*, translated by Eric Mosbacher and James Strachey. New York: Basic Books.

——. 1962a. "The Aetiology of Hysteria." *Standard Edition of the Complete Psychological Works of Sigmund Freud*, 3: 208-09. London: Hogarth Press.

——. 1962b. "Heredity and the Aetiology of the Neuroses." *Standard Edition of the Complete Psychological Works of Sigmund Freud*, 3: 142-56. London: Hogarth Press.

——. 1962c. "Further Remarks on the Neuro-psychoses of Defence." *Standard Edition of the Complete Psychological Works of Sigmund Freud*, 3: 159-85. London: Hogarth Press.

Jung, Carl. 1953. *Two Essays on Analytical Psychology. Collected Works* 7. New York: Pantheon Books.

——. 1961. *Freud and Psychoanalysis. Collected Works* 4. New York: Pantheon Books.

——. 1967. *Symbols of Transformations. Collected Works* 5. Princeton, New Jersey: Princeton University Press.

Nietzsche, Frederick. 1901. *Werke Grossoktavausgabe* 3. Leipzig: Kroner

Chapter 4

Reduction/Finalism and the Child

Patricia Berry

During the past few years I have found myself reflecting increasingly on my childhood. But this time my thoughts are less imaginative and hypothetical. Now they are more tightly causal and determinative. I am thinking as though my current situations actually derive from events in my childhood in ways that are unambiguous and conclusive. Jung regards this as reductive thinking, and I cannot believe I am doing it.

Jung equates reductive thinking with causal thinking. He generally does not distinguish between the two, and so I also will be using them interchangeably. Causality, Jung sees as a perspective toward events. He does not make the mistake of regarding causality and its results as either true or false, but rather regards causal thinking as a more or less useful way of seeing (It is most useful when one sees things that one would not see otherwise.) (Jung 1969, 8: paragraph 6). Causal thinking tends to be mechanistic, machine-like — this trips that — and linear, unidirectional (*a* causes *b* causes *c* — Newton's billiard balls) — *x* in the past causes *y* in the present. Jung does not tend to think of causality as reversible or very complicated. More precisely, that is not when Jung uses the term "causal." He does not speak of what is now called "top-down" causality. When he is pointing to more complicated connections, he uses terms like "synchronicity" or "finality."

The causal perspective, according to Jung, leads to a uniformity of meaning. It is simplistic. Many different nuances are reduced to one explanation. It does not take into account the contingencies, richness, and complexity of psychological phenomena, or that part of psychological phenomena that is more than the simply personal, simply biographical.

Furthermore, the causal, reductive approach, according to Jung, leads to fixed meanings. An event in the past (or a symbol) tends to mean one thing and one thing only. It does not shift with context or over time. There are no levels of meaning, little duplicity or irony. Also, significance tends to be cloaked, concealed. Things are not as they appear on the surface, but meaning is something hidden that must be got to. Meaning is disguised in the welter of phenomena that must be penetrated.

Jung contrasts this mechanistic, causal point of view with what he calls finalistic or constructive (or purposive or teleological). When one looks at things finalistically, one looks for intrinsic value in an event or image or whatever. One sees things as striving toward a goal, as having a sense of purpose, as teaching something. (Jung says one learns things one did not know before when perceiving finalistically.)

When one compares the description of these two modes of thinking, it is clear which is better. (The causal is mechanistic, reductive, simplistic, fixed; whereas the final opens up — is purposive and constructive, gives value, and moves into the future.)

This finalistic perspective was an important contribution of Jung to the psychological thinking of his time. It was part of his genius. Even in his earliest psychiatric writings, he shows this attitude of purposefulness regarding psychological phenomena. Though this attitude was part of Jung's genius, nonetheless, as we all know, Jung also allowed place for causal thinking. It was useful, he said, for dealing with persons in the first half of life, getting to the objective level of the dream, resolving the transference, getting to the shadow, dealing with "reality" and simple instincts, and so on.

Nonetheless, I find that when I feel myself operating in a particularly Jungian manner, I am generally not thinking in a reductive or causal way. I am not tracing present emotions to personal events in a reductive manner, not reducing them to traumas.

However, I am aware that what may feel particularly Jungian to me, in my practice, need not be necessarily what feels Jungian to other practitioners. For myself, when I feel most Jungian, I sense this push from behind, urging me to go deeper than what is first apparent, a push to recognize ambiguity, duplicity, shadows.

I am aware of different viewpoints, multiple perspectives that can be brought to bear. I am cautioned to be suspicious of what is simply collective or current so that I always have one foot outside collective phenomena. Furthermore, as a Jungian, I see things intrapsychically as well as interpsychically, interpersonally. And my attitude toward symptoms, events, and symbols is purposive. I see them as meaningful beyond anything they might be reduced to, as having value, as attempts to move toward something.

When I feel my most Jungian self, I often feel it in distinction to a more Freudian way of viewing — not strange since Jung himself emphasized the distinction. Jung was creating Jung. In doing so, it was important to distinguish his methods from those of Freud. Also, this is how many of us learned Jung — in contrast to Freud. Freud's ideas were simplistic and reductive; Jung's were complex and expansive. Freud was narrow and personal, while Jung was broad and archetypal. Freud talked about object cathexis, Jung about growth and wholeness. That was Jungian. That is why we went to Zurich. That is why we wanted a Jungian analysis. That is why our analysands come to us.

What has happened in our field in recent years is that many of us have become increasingly interested in the child and child-hood. (There are Jungian training programs in child psychology and Jungian conferences on the child.) And with this increased interest has come, of course, developmental thinking, as well as a certain concern regarding personal biography. What is, or was, the role of the parents? The siblings? What were the causal influences on the personal psyche of the child? Though most of this is done in a way that incorporates Jungian understandings, still there is more emphasis on biographical details and their influence — hence causal thinking — than has been customary in most Jungian circles.

This interest in the events of childhood and their causal signif-icance parallels a trend in the collective as well. I am thinking here of mainstream psychotherapy — psychotherapy as it is taught in social work schools and counselling psychology programs. In these mainstream approaches, the child is looked to for etiological significance. Childhood events are of great concern for the causal role they play in the adult psyche. Incest, sexual trauma, and physical and emotional abuse shape the child, according to these approaches, and, consequently, the child in the adult.

Collectively, this is a time of the child. Adults are now "adult children," victims of dysfunctional patterns and pathological family situations over which they had, as children, no control. This image of the child as victim — abused, powerless — portrays the child as basically innocent in a Rousseauian sense. The problem is not in the child's own nature, but comes with the events to which the child has been subjected.

This view of the child has a different coloration from Freud's view, where we see the child as one with libidinous impulses of the id, polymorphously perverse, omnipotent with desire. Freud's is a more powerful child, a child not only a victim of outer forces, but also wrestling with an internal world of built-in conflict. Jung's child, too, is richly complicated internally. The collective unconscious offers an abundance of archetypal dominants to consider along with the realities of an environmental situation. Furthermore, Jung's child is not wholly a victim of its environment for it has archetypal help. The *mundus imaginatis* gives alternatives that can nurture in even the most atrocious familial, environmental situations.

Certainly, these models of the child — Freud's, Jung's, the model current in the collective — portray important phenomenological aspects of the archetype. Indeed, the child is innocent, as well as libidinous, omnipotent; victimized, as well as imaginative, creative. But what is causing the trouble is what is most important to hear (as with any other symptom). What is claiming itself most important is the child as victim. It is as though the collective child is saying: "See me as victim. I'm abused. I'm powerless. See me!"

We have no choice but to see. But for me (and my kind of Jungian), it has not always been easy to accept this victimized child simply on its own terms. One of the problems is that it is only a piece of an archetype — the victimized piece. What about the other parts? — the child as indulgent, deceitful, creative, resourceful, imaginative, tyrannical? Furthermore, the child's claim is part of a collective movement. And, as Jungians, we tend to be suspicious of collective movements.

So these are two difficulties. One is that the victimized child is identifying with only part of the archetype. Thus, there is a splitting of the archetype and a projection of the shadow elsewhere onto parents, family, adults. Also, insofar as this identification is part of a collective contagion, it is a mass movement that is unconscious and, given Jung's warnings, potentially as dangerous as any other mass movement.

It is easy for me to use my Jungian awareness to explain away this victim phenomenon as simply splitting and a defense on a collective level. However, so doing, I block myself from taking it seriously. (I see it reductively, as "nothing but" a defense.) Here is where Jung's finalistic attitude becomes crucial. Though identification with the victimized child may be a symptom, the finalistic question would be: "what is the value of that symptom?" What is it pointing toward?

One of the reasons we may not automatically think this way is because Jung made rather clear distinction between causality and finality, as I detailed in the beginning of this essay. In this case, viewing identification with the child in the manner we just have (as a split archetype, a collective contagion) has been reductive. We have said it was nothing but a splitting and an identification. We have explained it away simplistically, leaving aside any sense of purposiveness about the phenomenon itself. This is a Jungian reduction — this tendency to explain away in the negative, saying that is its purpose. Its purpose is to avoid. That is not what Jung meant by finalism, as I understand it.

And in any case, it is important to remember that a distinction made about modes of thinking/perceiving need not be a split in the phenomenon itself. It is all too easy to explain away something as unpsychological or collective and to polarize it with something one considers more psychological and "the right way" (as though anything really could be "un"psychological). What I would urge here is that we return psychological value to victim identification and ask what is going on.

One of the things about finalism, by the way, is that we are not going to know for sure what is going on. If we did, it would be prophecy, or what Jung warns against as teleology (Jung 1969, 8: paragraph 3, note 4) (theology in the telos) — a worked out system, a logos, regarding the literal future of things. As I understand it, finalism is about an attitude, a valuing, a giving credit.

If we give this kind of value, then it is apparent that identification with the child-as-victim is a necessary psychological experience. Perhaps it is necessary in moving the psyche into an emotional place from which process and transformation can then occur.

Is the victimized child like a repressed aspect, a victim of culture itself? Or a victim of the developments, the refinements of the modern age? Is it like the dregs, the material remaining at the base of the container after transformation? The orphan left unparented after the coniunctio? Could it be that much of our psychic development (I am speaking here intrapsychically, not only intrapsychically, but personally) — could it be that much of my psychological development proceeded at the expense of a child-like, vulnerable orphan, not only a victim of my own life, but a victim of the process of analysis itself?

What drew many of us so powerfully to Jungian psychology was its broad cultural vision. It offered a way of seeing individual hurts in a less personal and more purposive light. There was the promise — and the reality — of transformation. But could it be that the shadow effect of these transformations, these refinements, was to leave behind dregs that were apparently only personal, buried in the mundane details of my merely personal biography (my own actual mother, not the archetypal one, and all the compensations and richness that brought; my own lack of father, not its cultural and archetypal replacements)? Somehow, things got accepted, turned positive, productive, and transformed perhaps too skillfully (maybe through amplification into wider contexts, maybe by a too immediate use of the finalistic perspective). So it is for this personal reason — my own untransformed piece, the orphan in me, the victimized child of my own development — that I present these remarks.

Now identifying myself as victim, I have radically reduced who I am and what I am about. I have put my ability and accomplishments aside for the sake of another round in the container, another operation. I have made myself *prima materia*.

One of the puzzling aspects of this phenomenon of victimization is the struggle that so many individuals go through trying to determine whether the abuse in their childhood occurred as an event in fact, or not. For many of my analysands, this is a crucial question. Did my father, mother, uncle, babysitter, or caretaker abuse me, or am I just making this up?

My own attitude here is that it does not matter crucially. In my Jungian soul, I feel that what is experienced emotionally or imaginally has occurred psychologically, and that is plenty to work with. Visions, dreams, fantasies, and active imaginations are real and, in fact, "create reality" as Jung says. Not so for my analysands. Not so for the culture in general. For the more factual mind, it makes a great difference whether something is factually, as distinct from emotionally, real. So my analysands go to great lengths trying to remember, and then trying to distinguish whether what they remember is fact or fantasy. Much of the literature regarding this question of physical abuse, by the way, counsels that if one has the personality traits of one who has been abused (lack of self esteem, difficulty trusting, a tendency to dissociate), then it is safe to assume one has been.

I personally think that sexual contact between adults and children is probably rather common. Because of this assumption and my impatience to get on with the therapy, I frequently find myself saying to analysands things like "let's assume it did, and go on from there."

But I have to be careful. If my tone betrays a hint of metaphor or that I am not taking this event as completely, literally, factually true — then we are in for another round of "did it" or "did it not" occur? It is as though the abused child requires a direct and literal response in order to ground and make real its emotion.

We talk of emotion as being one with the child, but the child also easily loses its emotion — it gets distracted, it forgets, it adapts. To hold an emotion over time, consciously and consistently, is actually a developmental achievement. So the child needs help in holding its emotion. Simplicity, singularity, literalism, and reduction are such helps.

We live in a complicated age. Certainly, the sociopolitical world is complex, and the internal psychological world, with its multifaceted, multileveled possibilities of awareness, is even more so. This complexity is overwhelming for the child who has been left behind, the orphan in the container. Relativity, perspectivism, hermeneutics, as if awareness, deconstructionism, systemic thought — are delightful sophistications for the adult mind, but they are confusing to the child's.

The child asks for certainty (not ambiguity), stability, fixity, safety (not irony, duplicity, the double entendres of adult life). And this child exists in all of us — essentially so. For me, it is the dumbling, the one that does not get the joke, make the turn, or the shy one who clings to its mother's skirts, does not venture forth until it knows what is what. The literal gives this sense of what is what. And the literal is an illusion. No mother is there really (not entirely), no stability, no safety — except in the flux of what comes and goes.

But the illusion is important — even for the adult mind in its sophistication. As the child needs to come and go from its mother, mentally we, too, need fixed points (we call them basic assumptions, propositions, givens) from which our thinking can then venture forth, our theories be spun, our attitudes tried out. We need to invent these fixities in order to be safely and productively relative. It is all part of the game.

Another aspect of the child's insistence upon the literal — what is or was an event, in fact or not — has to do, I think, with body, by which I mean psychic substance, being, the sense of one's self as a concrete organism, substantially living, breathing, feeling, and moving.

The abused child experiences its body through the damage that has been done to it. By reliving scenes of abuse, the child experiences not only the abuse, but also the body as such. What I am suggesting is that perhaps psychic body in this day and age is an abused body, so that psychologically or emotionally getting in touch with body is at once getting in touch with the abused, the violated — that that is body. And so the cry of our victimization is a cry returning us to body as it is.

The awareness that I am suggesting is an awareness by means of *mortificatio,* an awareness through suffering — an awareness that becomes more real, the more literal it is imagined to be. Therapeutically, this suggests that, at times, it may be important to imagine things as even more literal than may be the case. This way of proceeding is quite different from what I have generally assumed to be psychological.

In the past, I have assumed the ability to reflect as essential to psychological awareness — cognizance of shadow, the realization of other levels in what was going on, duplicity. Awareness of shadow is, according to Jung, the first stage of the psychological process. I always ascribed to that.

Now I am thinking that perhaps there is another way as well, a way that proceeds from the literal to the more literal. When this process is called for, shadow awareness is not the point at all — in fact, it interferes. Shadow awareness shortcircuits the possibility of identifying as victim. Instead of intensifying the experience by making it more literal and thus arriving at the experience of body, shadow awareness dissolves identification and so, in this case, the experience of psychic body.

For example, someone comes in saying that he/she has been abused. If I am thinking in terms of the shadow, I immediately look for where the person is abusing themselves (inter or intra psychically) and then projecting the problem. Or I look for how they are setting up situations in terms of abuse/non-abuse through the structures and myths they are living. To the extent that I follow this track therapeutically, I will be helping dissolve their too singular identification as victim.

But suppose that my intent is the opposite — to simplify and intensify the identification, to coagulate instead of dissolve it. Then I will ask leading, reductive questions — questions meant to intensify the identification and the experience of abuse. Who abused you? What happened? I will work to pull out as many feelings as possible around that abuse and to explore how these feelings reverberate in the present.

This use of reduction is something we all employ at times in the course of doing therapy. (It has to do with making an emotion more real.) What I am urging here is merely that we be aware of this tool as a tool — that we recognize its value and use it consciously, alchemically, for a particular effect.

Barbara Walters is brilliant at this, by the way. How did you feel? Why did you do this? Were you sad over your father's death, the breakup of your marriage, the loss of your child? She asks, intrusively. But the effect is that it goes straight to the child, and the child responds to reductive questions with its own condensed, concretized emotion.

To summarize, I have explored the importance of reduction for dealing with the child. I have said that causal thinking evokes the child and childlike emotionality through its very simplicity, that

that is its purpose. In other words, from a finalistic point of view, the importance of reduction is to ground the psyche and its relativity in the more simplistic certitude of the child. Literalism aids that certitude — the psyche as actual event, actual traumas, memories — singular, without duplicity, irony, or levels. To the child's mind, only one thing can be true at a time. This simplicity provides necessary grounding in a world that is, indeed, ambiguous and complex. To be innocent, the child without blame, an abused victim, brings the child to an experience of body that is the *prima materia* from which psychological work can then proceed.

Another characteristic of the child in our time is that it does not exist alone. This is a time of relations. Things exist relative to, in relation with, other things. The child develops in relation with objects (object relations), and as part of, in relation with, systems — most particularly the family system.

Family therapy todays is generally influenced by systems theory (a result of Gregory Bateson's reflections, promulgated most prominently by the Milan school). When a family is viewed systemically, its members are seen as radically interconnected. That means that a change in any one member necessitates change in the family as a whole since everyone is interdependently part of the same web. Persons are seen as playing roles in the family (scapegoat, hero, and comic) in order to serve the family system and keep it intact. Thus, to create change in the family or to heal any of its members, the therapist need not focus necessarily on the individual who has the symptom, but might focus on any member of the system since any change will affect the whole. (In fact, one of the techniques is to focus not on the sick member, but on the person most likely to be able to change.)

So in the systemic view, every individual is necessarily related with, and dependent on, every other individual within the system. One is born into a family with the urge or the instinct to serve. There is an implicit, basic love not only for one's parents, but for one's siblings and the system itself — even if serving this love requires a psychosis or eating disorder.

Jung's view of the family is quite different. Rather than an interdependent whole, the family, for Jung, is more a collection of individuals — individuals who may, at various times, be in participation mystique, but who essentially each have individual challenges, unique myths, and destinies to work out — if, that is, they are marked for individuation, to be unique individuals, not just part of the collective herd.

Now this attitude in Jung (which has been called elitist) is not the only attitude in Jung, or even what he really means by individuation. I think most of us would agree that, in the end, the more deeply one is connected with the Self, the more deeply one is also connected with others. Also, as Jungians we certainly do not regard ourselves as unrelated individuals. From the beginning, we are part of a profound and very large family — the family of "man," of humanity. The collective unconscious, the archetypes, are sources of support and interconnection. And this collective unconscious is at least as, if not more, determinative than the merely personal, biological family through which it is filtered.

But there is a shadow to our emphasis upon the individual and individuation. (The shadow can take hold of anything. There is something in all of us that tends to take especially the theory we embrace and turn it into a defense justifying our weaknesses and avoiding what may be personally difficult or threatening).

When individuation is taken hold of in this way, we get a splitting and an antipathy — a splitting upward, so one part becomes superior, the other inferior: the individual versus the collective, the unique versus the familial, the archetypal versus the common, the special versus the ordinary.

Now the child, or the aspect of the child, that has been dominant in Jungian psychology until recently seems to have been the "special" or divine child. I am thinking here of that heroic child with partly divine parentage (one parent is a god). And the child is born in lowly, difficult circumstances. But because he has a special parent (or special, secret lineage), he is destined to achieve far beyond, and in spite of, the lowly circumstances of his birth and surroundings.

There are a number of possible ends to this myth. One is that the hero brings back to the culture the fruits of his labors and/or another is that he be destroyed by the collective forces or the "other gods" from which he has polarized himself in his struggles.

The kind of child currently asserting its voice in the collective is of a different sort. This child does not leave parents and home for the sake of more spiritually transformative or soul-connected forces. Rather, it insists upon connection with its actual parents, no matter how bad they were. In fact, because they were so bad, this child expends great effort remembering and reliving the wrongs that were "perpetrated" — which is, as we discussed earlier, a stage of its healing. My point here is that the child current in the culture insists on being related, and suffering that relationship to its actual parents and the actual concrete, traumatic, familial situations to which it was exposed.

Again, I think this child has something to teach us. Whereas our child has been divine — its shadow perhaps effete, "special," and isolationist — the child of the present day is obviously demanding, embroiled, simplistic, blaming, living its shadow, and adamantly relational in doing so. Is it not the shadow of our Jungian child that has led many of us as analysts into the self-contained domain of our highly individualized practices? The image I have here is of the isolated analyst in a private, therapeutic tower, narcissistically (though innocently, unconsciously) living out power needs in the shelter of this isolation.

This image is a caricature and not necessarily only Jungian, and it certainly does not refer to any of us here. Except it does refer to me because for many years I did involve analysands in my life for my own needs — things like giving me rides to airports, lending a hand with this or that, providing useful information — simply because I was unaware I was doing anything unusual or harmful. In the past years, I have cleaned up my act considerably (at least become more conscious of what I am doing while I am doing it) because I have seen the kinds of binds that can result for the child.

The unconsciousness of using one's analysands is a shadow that many in Jungian psychology are addressing. We have learned much about boundaries, ethics, and so on. These transgressions did not use to cause a stir. We did not talk about boundaries. (I had never heard the word until fifteen or so years ago). That is because the child is different from what it used to be.

The modern child constellated in our analysands and trainees — that child speaks up. It demands safety, protection, containment. It blows the whistle on what it considers abusive. My child did not do that or even feel that it was being abused. And I suspect it is the same for many people (which is what makes some of the current "ethical" situations so confusing).

The child in ourselves (that we went through analysis with) did not feel abused. We were in a different myth. What if Christ had felt abused, or Moses, or Oedipus, or Hercules? If they had tried to "work it through" with their parents, they would never have got on with the story. That was the myth with which our child was identified. We felt the necessity to move on, to transform, to incorporate more impersonally and archetypally. We developed (in part) by learning to handle the peculiarities and personal weaknesses of our analysts.

The child who enters analysis today is quite another child, with apparently quite a different process. I will explore what that process and its telos might be.

I have viewed the collective child as existing in an interaction, a system, in relation. This is not to say these relations are good. In fact, they are the problem. And not only is the immediate "family of origin" the problem, but the longitudinal, the historical family (the parents of the parents and their brothers and sisters). A detailed geneogram can show how present problems are recurrences of situations from earlier generations — an interesting variation of Jung's early notion of a racial, here familial, unconscious.

In any case, family, however longitudinally extended, is the problem, the "dysfunctional family." And most families seem to be more or less dysfunctional — at least judging by the symptoms — a large portion of which now are addictive. Addictions are a major problem for our modern child. So not only is our child radically related to family, but it is also radically related to addictive substances and activities.

Addiction, as we know, is now construed quite broadly. One can be addicted not only to drugs, alcohol, and gambling (those were the old addictions), but now also to food, sex, relationships, work, love, activity, even novelty. Judging from current literature, most any human activity that tips beyond the moderate may be regarded as an addiction.

If we come from families in which any member was addicted in any of these ways, we are called "adult children." So, the child and addiction are closely related. If we are not addicted ourselves (which we probably are, given the range of possibilities), someone else in our family or extended family is, or has been. But even then, even if we cannot find anyone — if we have problems, we have obviously come from a dysfunctional family, and that is the same thing. The treatment is the same. So given this tautological tangle, it is safe to assume we are all "adult children" and that addiction figures in some way in our psychologies.

For addiction, there is therapy, the most pervasive form of which is, of course, the 12-step programs. (I urge those who have not attended one of these meetings to do so. They are a brilliant psychological invention and a profoundly moving human drama.) It has been obvious to me from the meetings that I have attended that what is being worked on, however, is not only the addiction (though that is the presenting complaint, that is why people go), but also relationship itself, through an elaborate set of rules and conventions operative during the meeting.

Participants are not to interrupt or ask questions, make comments, or in any way engage the person speaking. There is no "cross talk" (which is to say, no normal interaction). Rather, each person speaks of his or her struggles and sufferings from as deep a level as he or she is able/willing, and then that is simply left, that simply is.

The result of this process is that a new level of connection among persons is created indirectly, a joining by way of the commonality, the humanity of suffering itself. What was overly personal for the child in the bind with his parental images becomes an impersonal sense of connection through suffering — an *unus mundus* based on the commonality (perhaps even univer-sality) of despair. What I am saying is that within the collective itself, there is a therapeutic form, these 12-step programs, which, imagined alchemically, seen finalistically, are addressing and transforming the dilemma of the overly relational, traumatized, literalizing child of our time. I suppose what functions as the transformational symbol here is the "higher power" that is spoken of. The higher power (or the transformational powers of the Self, in our terms), born of a very personal, literal suffering, is at once superordinant, beyond any merely personal life.

As a postscript, I will reflect about the role of Jungian psychol-ogy, as I see it, vis-a-vis these collective psychotherapeutic move-ments. As Jungians, we have sophisticated and subtle awarenesses at our disposal. Unlike many of the psychotherapies on the scene today, we have the benefit of a substantial history and tradition.

We stand on the shoulders of giants — Freud, Jung, and others of visionary stature. Our depth psychological tradition has seen cultural developments come and go. We have seen syndromes appear and then disappear, or change into other syndromes. Ideas for treatment have shifted this way and that. Because of the cultural vision of our tradition, we have an appreciation of the relativity of collective movements, as well as a sense of the where and why of their appropriateness. We have a variety of stances and attitudes. We can be reductive when that is called for, or finalistic, or both, as I have been attempting in this essay.

We know a great deal about shadow. We know, unlike many other more mainstream psychologies, that everything that exists — every movement, attitude, person, stance, moment (our own psychology included) — exists with a shadow, and not just one shadow, but many shadowing possibilities. We are experts in shadow awareness, and we bring that expertise to every situation we view.

I see our task now to be that of looking yet again to our own shadows. Though I would not encourage us simply to get on the bandwagon of the collective, victim-identified child, I also do not believe we can ignore its psychological reality. When we look simply at the shadow of this child, it is easy to dismiss it. What we really need is an awareness of the shadow of shadow awareness.

Therefore, I would encourage a finalistic perspective when looking at collective phenomena, in order to see what is trying to be accomplished and what movements of the psyche may already be taking place.

Bibliography

Jung, C.G. 1969. *The Structures and Dynamics of the Psyche. Collected Works* 8. Princeton: Princeton University Press.

Chapter 5

Hermes-Mercurius and the Self-Care System in Cases of Early Trauma

Donald E. Kalsched

Introduction

Some years ago, an old joke was making the rounds in New York: "How many psychotherapists does it take to change a lightbulb?" The punch-line is: "only one, but the lightbulb has to want to change!" We all know from clinical practice how true this is — how difficult our work can be if a patient (like the proverbial lightbulb) does not want to change. Nonetheless, we work with many such patients, and in some cases their resistance is so powerful that it feels like a basic instinct — apparently, an instinct for self-preservation. For these patients, the so-called "process of individuation" as Jung described it — based upon the differentiation and integration of psychic opposites — can seem like a faraway dream. These patients are allergic to psychic opposites and to the "wholeness" that might come from their integration. They cannot "own" shadow-material as a neurotic patient can. To ask them to do so is equivalent to asking them to swallow deadly poison. Closer examination of these patients' backgrounds reveals that, for them, normal ego growth was interrupted by early experiences of incapacitating anxiety — anxiety of sufficient magnitude to be justifiably called traumatic. Consequently, in place of normal development and the flexible structuring of the psychic apparatus that comes through the individuation process, archetypal defenses come into play, and, in alliance with the patient's brittle and rigid ego, these defenses are both primitive and refractory. Indeed, we might say that the more traumatically injured the patient, the stronger the resistances to change.

Despite the fact that these resistant patients are suffering and have sought our help to alleviate this suffering, they have an uncanny knack for getting themselves into situations which

94

undermine therapeutic progress and result only in intensified suffering — sometimes to the point of retraumatization. And yet these patients are not just stubborn, lazy, or masochistic. They themselves often feel helpless in the grip of their resistances and chagrinned at their seemingly perverse, almost "fated," repetitions of self-destructive behavior. On an ego level, they often wish to cooperate with the analytic process, but then, just on the threshold of some hopeful improvement, something subtle, trickster-like in their unconscious, attacks their newfound confidence and seduces them into yet another spell of forgetfulness or yet another repetition of self-destructive acting out, or yet another retreat into the haze of addiction.

By calling this intrapsychic factor "trickster-like," I have indicated "who" I think is archetypally responsible for this perverse resistance — none other than the patron saint of our depth psychology himself, Hermes Mercurius (!), albeit in what Jung calls his "underworld form" (Jung 1967, 13: paragraph 231). In this essay, I will be setting forth the idea that Hermes-Mercurius what might be described as an archetypal self-care system which accounts for the fierce resistance to individuation that we find in patients who have suffered early trauma. By trauma, I mean unbearable levels of anxiety in connection with certain childhood experiences, the "memory" of which threatens to revive this anxiety and is therefore dissociated.

In the unconscious of these patients, we find a figure who personifies these dissociative activities, and Hermes-Mercurius is an apt designation for such defensive processes. We usually think of Mercurius as an agent of mediation and integration, as well as the union of opposites. But in the unconscious material of patients suffering early trauma, we find an intrapsychic Mercurial factor which actually tries to split the opposites and annihilate integrative connections. Here, we have the diabolical aspect of our Janus-faced God. The word "diabolical" comes from the Greek *dia-bollein*, meaning "to tear apart," and serves as the antonym of *sym-bollein*, meaning "to pull together" (Murray 1897) which is Mercurius' other face.

In his diabolical form, Mercurius attacks the inner world, tears it apart, or tries to dissolve it *(solutio)* in altered states of oblivion in order to keep it away from unbearable anxiety. So, according to my hypothesis, while Mercurius performs an often diabolical function, our trickster-god is "trying," so to speak, to assure the survival of the whole personality. Envisioning Mercurius in this way enables us to think about the archetypal dimension of psychological defenses — a way of seeing the "God" in what for Freud were primarily "ego-defenses." I hope that these ideas will become clearer against the backdrop of some theory and a clinical vignette.

History of the Problem in the Literature of Freud and Jung

Freud himself was very puzzled by his patients' resistances: one in particular intrigued him — he called it the "negative therapeutic reaction." He noted that when the therapist spoke hopefully to certain patients or expressed satisfaction with their progress, they invariably became worse. Freud concluded: "there is something in these people that sets itself against their recovery" (Freud [1923] 1973a, 49). In other words, an unconscious, intrapsychic "complex" functions in these people as an active, inner agency, seemingly trying to prevent hope, growth, and individuation. Freud called this "daemonic" inner agency of the mind the "severe super-ego" and emphasized that in patients with a masochistic disposition, it became a truly sadistic punishing force, compelling the helpless ego of its victim to repeat self-destructive behavior in a "repetition compulsion," leading to continual retraumatization. So severe was this diabolical "force" in the unconscious of some patients that Freud was led to the pessimistic conclusion that it represented the internalized aggression of a "death instinct" — Thanatos (Freud [1920] 1973b, 118-19).

I do not know whether Jung would have agreed with the notion of a "death instinct." Certainly, the "archetypal shadow" or the "dark side of God" played an essential role in Jung's thinking about psychic opposites and the often-resisted human suffering necessary to unite them. More than any other psychological writer, it was Jung who left us with an impassioned and deeply meaningful analysis of the "shadow-problem" for collective man.[1] But Jung rarely talked about archaic destructiveness in the clinical domain. He usually discussed the problem of evil as an aspect of the Godhead (as in "Answer to Job"), or as an archetypal image collectively possessing a whole nation (as in his essay, "Wotan" [1947]). After the break with Freud, when Jung's own dreams contained rageful destructive imagery, such as rivers of blood or the murder of a beloved hero by a dark skinned savage, he was inclined to rationalize such imagery as a premonition of World War I, or the "necessary death" of his "heroic attitude" (1961, 180-81). Jung came closest to describing a negative, self-attacking agency in the psyche with his idea of the "negative animus," but this destructive inner imago was kept comfortably at arm's length as a problem of female psychology.[2] We also know that Jung sometimes behaved in very destructive and self-destructive ways with patients,[3] so we might wonder whether he ever really dealt adequately with his own destructive aggression, and whether, therefore, he could leave us a theory that would help us deal with ours.

Since Jung's original work, many of his followers have elaborated his notion of the "negative animus" and its archetypal forerunners. In American Jungian circles, this demonic figure is achieving a noteworthy popular recognition in the best-selling work of Linda Leonard (1990), in which "she" appears as the "Madwoman ... at the very heart of addiction," and as the main subject in Leonard's recent best-selling book, *Meeting the Madwoman* (1993), where she is described as an archetypal figure who is paradoxically (like Mercurius) both destructive or potentially creative. Another best-selling Jungian writer, Clarisa Pinkola Estes, in her recent *Women Who Run With The Wolves*, describes a masculine demon in women's psyches, known as the "Innate Predator" (1992, 44), analogous to Bluebeard in the fairy tale, representing a kind of "anti-life" force in the psyche, consistent with that unanalyzable bit of evil described by Marie-Louise von Franz (1974).

However, I think Hermes-Mercurius is a better archetypal candidate for this creative/destructive energy in the psyche than any of the others mentioned. Among other advantages, this gets us around the contradictory findings regarding the gender-identity of this inner figure. Leonard says this destructive inner agency is feminine (the Mad Woman) — Pinkola Estes sees it as masculine, an animus figure. Mercurius is both — ambisexual — altogether in keeping with his/her nature as a *complexio oppositorum*. Jung points out that he frequently appears in hermaphroditic form (1967, 13: paragraph 319).

Finally, to complete my review of the Jungian approach to this destructive inner factor, Michael Fordham suggests in an early essay that certain patients' negative therapeutic reactions might represent archaic "defenses of the Self" (1974, 192-99). Fordham did not discuss an inner personification of this negative imago, but he brought in the useful idea of archetypal defense. To this end, he made use of an earlier contribution by Leopold Stein, who hypothesized that archetypal defensive operations were analogous to the body's immunological reactions and occurred on a much deeper level than ego-defenses. Stein suggested that just like in auto-immune disease of the body, primitive aggressive energies can attack elements of the ego from within, resulting in self-destruction (1967, 103).

Clinical Example

Imagine the following situation. I am sitting with a middle-aged Catholic woman, an ex-nun, now a pediatric nurse, named Mary, who has been in analysis for several years, seeking relief from chronic depression, compulsive eating, and total anesthesia of sexual feelings. Despite her depression, Mary has a diverting sense of humor and an almost impregnable pleasing Persona that makes asking for help in therapy very difficult. On this particular day, as she settles herself into the chair opposite me, I am aware of feeling expectant and hopeful because of a "breakthrough" we have had in the previous hour. And yet, Mary's eyes are averted. Her face is bloated, her hair uncombed, and her skin blotchy. She is having trouble breathing. I am starting to worry about what has happened.

In the previous three months of her analysis, Mary had suffered the loss of a close friend, and with the help of the depressed affect that followed this loss, we had started piecing together painful fragments of a forgotten childhood, which heretofore had been described as idyllic. With the aid of pictures from the family album and talks with her parents, a picture was emerging which was much darker than expected. Mary discovered that she had toilet trained herself at age one and that she had been a "perfect child" from then on, growing up very fast, never complaining, and becoming the "Mommy" for her depressed mother's brood of seven more children. A great sadness enveloped these memories, as Mary slowly realized that she had been totally unable to depend on anyone and that, while cared for physically, emotionally she had been abandoned. During this period of analytic exploration, she had the following dream image:

> I see a little girl floating away from a space ship without an umbilical cord, arms outstretched in terror, eyes and mouth distorted in a desperate cry for Mommy.

When Mary allowed herself to feel this frightening image, her grief was overwhelming, and, typically, she felt shortness of breath in the session, just like the asthma she had suffered as a child. Each time we approached this anxiety and despair, she would need to cut off her feeling, sometimes with a sarcastic remark, or by "going blank." To complicate the matter, I was leaving in a month for vacation, and Mary had begun to realize for the first time and, to her horror, that she was feeling very dependent on me and was already missing me! She thought this was inappropriate and "sick."

In the previous hour when the "breakthrough" had occurred, Mary had very courageously acknowledged how vulnerable and dependent she felt, and then very sheepishly, even shamefully, and after many detours, she had asked if she might be in touch with me over the break if she needed to be. I had agreed with this, and for the first time, her otherwise stoical facade melted, and her eyes filled up with tears. We discussed the realities of how this phone contact would work, and, of course she said, she would never abuse it, and I said that I knew she would not. We parted that day, both very moved, and with a mutual feeling of intimacy and hope.

So why, in the follow-up session, was Mary looking so wretched, I wondered. "What's the matter?" I asked her. With great shame and fear of my disapproval, she then reported that immediately upon leaving the previous session, tears still in her eyes from our interchange, she had stopped at a bakery, purchased a whole chocolate cake and a quart of ice cream, gone home in state of possession, with her heart pounding, and eaten everything in one sitting. Five hours later, upon awakening from a stuperous

sleep, she had gone out to the "7-11," bought more food, and
consumed that also. The more she ate, the less satisfied she felt,
yet with each mouthful of food, there arose in her an agitated
desperation for more, until finally she collapsed exhausted,
"totally spaced out," in a despair that was painfully familiar. The
pattern, Mary lamented, was truly "perverse."

As we both sat in stunned silence, with me processing my
counter-transference disappointment — even irritation — she
said:

> You know, it's exactly like I'm possessed by the devil. Food is
> the only sensual pleasure I have. It's the only place I can lose
> control. I savor each spoonful of chocolate like it's the touch
> of a lover. I'm compelled to do it. I search it out — there's a
> feeling of dark excitement just approaching the bakery! The
> devil says "C'mon — you've done all this work, why don't you
> be bad for once — you need this. There's no sense fighting it
> Mary. It's hopeless! I'm too strong for you. You can always lose
> the weight. Right now you need this comfort. You're going to
> eat this and you know it. I want you all to myself. Leave your
> world behind and come into my world. You know how good it
> tastes, how good it feels. C'mon, Mary. You belong to me.
> Good girls don't say no!"

One can imagine my shock and dismay hearing this erotic
language from my very heretofore non-sexual patient. Who was
this speaking through her? Certainly not her otherwise "innocent," ingratiating ego, busy pleasing people all the time. This was
truly an aggressive and sensual part of her that I had known nothing about. And "he" was clever, sly, and manipulative. He used
the truth about her excessive "goodness" (which she was discovering in therapy) to seduce her into being "bad." But his version of
"bad" was regressive — a submission to addictive self-soothing by
ice cream, without risk — a substitute for the real surrender of ego
control in relationship with all of its attendant anxiety, shame,
and potential sexual feelings — precisely what Mary was beginning to experience in the transference.[4]

Mary also reported a dream that she had the night after the
binge:

> I'm checking into a hospital with my friend Patty (who is a
> much younger, very innocent, new nurse on her service).

We're there for some kind of procedure, maybe a blood test or something. I'm not sure. It's all very high-tech with many machines etc. The doctor in his white coat is very nice as he introduces us to the hospital. But as we walk down the hall to the place our blood will be drawn I begin to feel uneasy because there is something wrong with the other patients. They're all in a trance or something — like zombies. Their essence has been removed. I realize that we've been tricked! The doctor has lured us into a trap. The place is like a concentration camp! Instead of testing our blood he is going to inject us with a serum that will make us zombies too. I have this hopeless feeling that there is no way out of this. No one can hear us. There are no phones. I think "Oh my God, Mommy will die and they won't be able to let me know!" (Her mother was seriously ill at the time of the dream.) I hear the doctor's footsteps coming down the hall and I wake up in a sweat.

Interpretation of Clinical Material

So here we have a sequence of historical and psychological "events," in which I hope to uncover some meaning — first, we have the early traumatic abandonment that Mary and I were uncovering, then the dream of the terrified motherless baby fading into space that appeared in connection with this exploration, then the "breakthrough" of forbidden dependency feelings in the transference, the violent resistance to this implied in the acting out of the food binge (with its seductive demonic voice), and, finally, the dream of the trickster doctor who seduces her into the zombie hospital and the accompanying thought that, "Mommy will die and ... I won't know it." I would ask the reader to hold these themes in mind while I briefly review some literature which both illuminates the case of Mary and provides "building blocks" for the Alchemical argument that I have outlined about Mercurius and the psyche's archetypal self-care system.

The Nature of Mary's Anxiety

To understand this case, it is necessary to examine the nature of Mary's anxiety. Both Winnicott and Kohut have pointed out that a certain level of "unthinkable" anxiety originates at a symbiotic stage of child development, where the child is totally dependent on the mother as a kind of external, metabolizing organ of psychological experience. The mother's role is to help mediate experience, and this means especially to help metabolize anxiety. It is as though the infant breathes in psychological oxygen through "lungs" supplied by the mother. What happens, then, when suddenly the mother is gone? Winnicott puts it this way:

> ... [for the baby] the feeling of the mother's existence lasts x minutes. If the mother is away more than x minutes, then the imago fades, and along with this the baby's capacity to use the symbol of the union ceases. The baby is distressed, but this distress is soon mended because the mother returns in x + y minutes. In x + y minutes the baby has not become altered. But in x + y + z minutes the baby has become traumatized. In x + y + z minutes the mother's return does not mend the baby's altered state. Trauma implies that the baby has experienced a break in life's continuity, so that primitive defences now become organized to defend against a repetition of "unthinkable anxiety" or a return to the acute confusional state that belongs to disintegration of nascent ego structure. We must assume that the vast majority of babies never experience the x + y + z quantity of deprivation. This means that the majority of children do not carry around with them for life the knowledge from experience of having been mad. Madness, here, simply means a breakup of whatever may exist at the time of a personal continuity of existence. After "recovery" from x + y + z deprivation, a baby has to start again, permanently deprived of the root which could provide continuity with the personal beginning (Winnicott 1971, 97).

In the case of Mary, the dream image that emerged of what must have been her long forgotten x + y + z deprivation was that of a little girl falling into space, her arms outstretched, eyes full of terror, her mouth distorted in a silent scream for Mommy, with no supply of oxygen — no connection to the mother ship. Anxiety over the lost mother-connection returns in the second dream, where she is trapped in the zombie hospital. Her central anxiety there is that her mother will die and she will not know it. Again, Winnicott has taught us that many dreads of this kind are really encoded memories of things that have already happened before full ego-formation (Winnicott 1989, 87-89), and if we apply this insight to Mary's dream, we might surmise that her mother's "death" is something that has already happened emotionally even though she does not "know it," and even though her actual mother is still alive. In other words, the zombie hospital is a "place" where she will be anesthetized to the loss of the mother — where she will lose all psychic connection to this fact. This will be assured by the trickster-doctor, who will administer his mind-altering serum.

Translated into Jungian language, we might say that an "unthinkable" level of anxiety results when archetypal energies fail to be humanized and the child is left at the mercy of the "terrible," as well as the "good," mother-archetype. But this language does not capture the emotional essence of this experience for the child who is now our patient. Heinz Kohut comes closer when he calls this anxiety "disintegration anxiety." It is, Kohut says, the "deepest anxiety man can experience" (1984, 16). It threatens the total annihilation of one's very humanity — the outright destruction of the human personality. To prevent this destruction, we might say that an archetypal "force" comes to the rescue. This archetypal "force" represents a self-care defensive system which is far more archaic and devastating than the more common level of "ego-defenses." Psychoanalysis calls these defenses "primitive" — especially splitting and projective identification. In Jungian language, we would call them archaic and typical, namely, archetypal defenses. One of the most remarkable things about these archetypal defenses is that in depth analytic work — with early trauma especially — we find them personified in the dream material, revealing themselves as an archaic "person" who apparently dismembers the patient's experience, in order to prevent the destruction of personality to which Kohut refers. This personified inner agency — "Mr. Dissociation" himself — is Hermes-Mercurius. We find him in Mary's material in two places — first as the diabolical "voice" of her food binge and, second, as the trickster-doctor, seducing her into the zombie hospital, where she will be forever separated from her life and from the mother's "death."

Two Kinds of Dissociation Associated With Two Levels of Anxiety

The disintegration anxiety which Mary carried inside her body is the kind of anxiety that we must imagine got its start in her very early life before a coherent ego was formed. So when this anxiety starts to come up again, it threatens to fragment the personality, and the nature of dissociation required to prevent this is more severe and archaic than the more "benign" forms of dissociation we associate with neurotic conflict. For the neurotic, the return of dissociated shadow-material creates anxiety, but this material can be recognized and integrated, leading to an inner *coniunctio oppositorum* and greater wholeness of personality. This is because the neurotic has a place within his psyche for repressed material.

It is different with the victim of early trauma. For these patients, disowned material is not psychically represented, but has been banished to the body or relegated to discrete psychical fragments, between which amnesia barriers have been erected. It must never be allowed to return to consciousness. A *coniunctio oppositorum* is the most terrifying thing of all, and the dissociation necessary to insure the patient against this catastrophe is a deeper split in the psyche. Jung himself alluded to these different levels of dissociation in his distinction between the kind of trauma that creates personal complexes and the kind of trauma that creates collective complexes:

> Certain complexes arise on account of painful or distressing experiences in a person's life, experience of an emotional nature which leave lasting psychic wounds behind them. A bad experience of this sort often crushes valuable qualities in an individual. All these produce unconscious complexes of a personal nature.... A great many autonomous complexes arise in this way.... But there are others that come from quite a different source ... the collective unconscious. At bottom they are irrational contents of which the individual had never been conscious before.... So far as I can judge, these experiences occur ... when something so devastating happens to the individual that his whole previous attitude to life breaks down (1967, 8: paragraph 314).

Jung then contrasts how we experience these two levels of the complex:

[If a complex from the personal unconscious is dissociated] ... the individual experiences a sense of loss [which for the primitive is equivalent to a loss of soul]. Conversely, when [such a] complex is made conscious again, for instance through psychotherapeutic treatment, he experiences an increase of power. Many neuroses are cured in this way. But when, on the other hand, a complex of the collective unconscious becomes associated with the ego ... it is felt as strange, uncanny ... fascinating ... even dangerous [Primitives experience this level of complex as possession by a spirit.] (Jung 1967, 8: paragraphs 311-12).

According to my hypothesis, the "possessing spirit" is precisely Mercurius, and he functions as an archetypal defense — an inner system of self-care — preventing the unthinkable traumatic anxiety from being experienced. In order to accomplish his necessary dismembering of experience, we might think of Mercurius as operating in two areas of experience. The first of these is the transitional space between the ego and the external world of reality. The second is the inner symbolic space between the ego and the internal world, the unconscious. In his diabolical form, Mercurius tries to sever the connections on both fronts. When operating between ego and world, his role is to encapsulate the personality in a kind of counter-dependent, self-sufficient bubble. Here, his protective, caretaking functions are more conspicuous. When operating between the ego and contents of the unconscious, Mercurius' role is to sever the links and connections within the psyche. Here, his aggressive, persecutory qualities are more obvious. I would like to look at both transitional areas as they pertain to my experience with Mary.

Attacks on Connections Between Inner and Outer Reality

Mercurius is the God found at all boundaries, borders, and threshold crossings, and so it stands to reason that he would be very active as a mediating (or non-mediating) function in that "transitional zone" between inner self and outer world — precisely the interface where Mary's traumatic anxiety was experienced before her ego had formed. Winnicott has helped us to understand that when "unthinkable" trauma occurs, the psyche splits, and there is a corresponding split in the "potential space," where the ego is alive between illusion and reality. This "transitonal space" is the "place" where the child learns how to play and how to use symbols. Repeated exposure to traumatic anxiety kills this symbolic activity and replaces it with what Winnicott calls "fantasying." Fantasying is a dissociated state, which is neither imagination, nor living in external reality, but a kind of melancholic self-soothing compromise which goes on forever — a defensive use of the imagination in the service of anxiety avoidance. My patient, Mary, lived in this "limbo" much of the time, sadly fantasying about, and idealizing, the mother she never really had — rewriting history to deny, at all costs, her underlying despair and fury.[5]

Masud Khan once said of patients like Mary:

> With the gravely ill person, one is rarely dealing, at first, with the authentic illness of the patient. What one has to negotiate some sort of alliance with is the patient's practice of self-cure, which is rigidly established by the time he reaches us. To treat this practice of self-cure merely as a resistance is to fail to acknowledge its true value for the person of the patient. It is my belief from my clinical practice that very few illnesses in a person are difficult to handle and cure. What, however, is most difficult to resolve and cure is the patient's practice of self-cure. To cure a cure is the paradox that faces us in these patients (1974, 97).

But Mary's self-cure and self-sufficiency was breaking down, and she was falling into what lay underneath it — abject feelings of resourceless dependency and the fragmentation anxiety associated with this dependency. She was being tempted out of her self-care cocoon by the possibilities emerging in the transference to allow herself to depend upon a real person, but the awareness of her own separateness which this entailed immediately brought in the shameful feelings and traumatic anxiety associated with her early abandonment. As an archetypal defender of her psyche, Mercurius saw this new anxiety-producing situation — considering it to be a renewed threat of the original trauma — and tried his best to prevent the unbearable anxiety from being experienced again. He did this by seducing her into the self-soothing oblivion of her food orgy. He was the voice of her food demon and a powerful trickster. In this case, he was stronger than Mary's transference to me, and the moment she left my office, she was under his spell, so to speak. Like all addictions, her food binge was part of Mary's self-care ritual, an elaborate effort to soothe herself, without ever letting on to anyone how empty she felt.

Edward Edinger has illustrated how the diabolical side of Mercurius functions in Alchemy, and there are many parallels with our case. Although we usually think of Mercurius as the mediating spirit of Alchemy's "Greater Coniunctio," representing a true combining of differentiated opposite substances into an uncorruptible third thing, he is also the instigator of what Edinger calls the "Lesser Coniunctio," representing the fusion of substances not yet completely separated (1985, 211-15). As ruler of the "Lesser Coniunctio," he appears as Hermes Kyllenios, a lascivious daemon, an oblivion-seeker overseeing the blissful "continuous cohabitation" of the naked couple in the Rosarium pictures (Jung 1967, 13: paragraph 231), leading not to rebirth, but to "dissolution" of the ego in addiction-like states — just like Mary's orgiastic food-binge. A common image of this "Lesser Coniunctio" is mother-son incest, where the son is cut to pieces (castrated) in the mother's embrace (Jung 1967, 14: paragraph 21). At this incestuous level of libido development, the immature ego is under the hypnotic spell of an unconscious undertow into non-differentiation. Levy Bruhl called this a state of "participation mystique." Psychoanalysts have named it "projective identification," where self and object are not clearly differentiated.

Although the "Lesser Coniunctio" is a normal developmental stage in the gradual differentiation and transformation of the psyche, it is possible to get stuck here. The archetypal self-care system provides the path of least resistance back into the "self-care" of Mercurius. Here, a retreat into "Oneness" replaces the hard work of separation necessary for "Wholeness."[6] We can see a "wisdom" in this regression and a "teleology," but not one with a happy outcome. In trying to protect Mary from an imagined re-traumatization in the transference, our Mercurial figure dissolves her ego in an orgiastic, compulsive ritual of submission until she has lost all awareness of her genuine need to depend on someone real and its accompanying anxiety. This is not regression, as we like to think of it in Jungian theory, for the purpose of renewal, but "malignant regression" (Balint 1979) — regression which suspends a part of her in a twilight state of dazed autohypnosis,[7] in order (so the Mercurial figure thinks) to assure the survival of herself as a human person. Yet the result is de-humanized living. True humanity depends upon the full tragi-comic interplay of life's opposites. But the psyche's archetypal auto-immune defenses cannot permit this. The innocent personal spirit of the patient must be protected at all costs.

In the dream material of the trauma victim, this personal spirit is sometimes represented as an innocent "child" or animal appearing in tandem with the caretaking side of our diabolical figure. Mercurius now appears as a kind of Guardian Angel,[8] who watches out for this innocent and cares for it (feeding it with substitutes), as long as the vulnerable creature never wants to leave its comfortable prison and emerge into the world (or come down into the body). Here, we have a structure in the psyche which is simultaneously infantile and very grown up, innocent and jaded at the same time. Those clinicians who have worked with people like Mary, who are embedded in the "Lesser Coniunctio," will confirm how utterly vulnerable, un-initiated, needy, and infantile these patients are on the one hand, and how haughty, inflated, arrogant, know-it-all, and resistant they are, on the other. This inflated inner defensive structure is like a "King-Baby" or "Queen Baby." It is extremely difficult for patients to give up these omnipotent inner objects in the absence of genuinely satisfying early experiences of dependency.[9]

We find this same structure represented frequently in mythology, as, for example in Rapunzel and her Witch, Snow White and the Wicked Stepmother, Bluebeard and his "innocent" wife, Yahweh and the children of Israel, or (in our dream) Mary and her simultaneously "nice"/evil doctor, who wants her in the concentration-camp hospital, cut off from the real world with its attendant anxiety and suffering.

As Edinger makes clear, the contaminated (inflated) mixtures of the Lesser Coniunctio are a first stage in the opus of individuation, which must be subjected to further procedures. Here is where analytic "head-shrinking" comes in. The grandiosity of the patient's self-care system must be sacrificed. The procedures in Alchemy which effect this painful transformation have to do with *mortificatio* and *separatio* and are frequently represented in Alchemy as death of the king or, alternatively, the sacrifice of an innocent baby or the Paschal lamb (Edinger 147-80).

As applied to our case, this means that Mary would have to give up her self-care illusions — the fantasy-world in which she and her mother existed in a kind of blissful dual union, bathed in goodness and innocent "love" — needing no one else, including her therapist. Into this "lesser coniunctio," she would have to let the horrific reality of her actual abandonment by her real mother — giving up the illusory "good" mother she never had. She would also have to mourn all the unlived life that her self-cure had prevented her from living. This would mean the dual sacrifice of both her God-like self-sufficiency and the innocent demands associated with it. In Melanie Klein's language, she would have to give up her manic defense and begin to mourn the loss of her objects, entering the "depressive position."

We know this process never happens without the release of alot of rage and aggression — and this is exactly what I was beginning to feel in my counter-transference reaction to Mary's food binge. We might say that I was beginning to wrestle with her Black Magician, our diabolical Mercurius. I could feel his grip on her and his hatred and suspicion of me. I could also "see" him in the diabolical doctor of Mary's zombie-hospital dream. I could see how he had lured the dream ego into an ostensible place of healing, now revealed as a concentration camp enclosure full of bloodless wraiths, their human essence removed, injected with dehumanizing "zombie-serum."[10]

The image of Mercurius as an inner murderer takes us to the second "area" where this archetypal defense is active — in the transitional space "inside" the psyche, between the ego and contents of the unconscious. In order to protect the nascent personality from further trauma, the inner figure we are discussing attacks all links between self and other (the area we have just explored), but also all integrative connections in the inner world. In other words, he attacks the very capacity for experience itself, which means "attacking the links"[11] between affect and image, perception and thought, sensation and knowledge. The result is that experience is rendered meaningless, coherent memory is "disintegrated," and individuation is interrupted. In the language of Mary's dream, the person becomes a zombie. We find this frightening inner fragmentation in cases of Multiple Personality Disorder. For the MPD patient, memory is available only as affect without image, or as breakthrough imagery without affect, or as disruptive bodily sensations, or as repetitive, self-destructive, behavior.

This is the perverse cost of Mercurius' "efforts" at protection. He protects by destroying, and, just like auto-immune disease in the body, his attack upon the self — based on mistakenly identifying a benign current situation for an earlier traumatic one — leads only to further destruction and despair. Jung says that Mercurius even drove the alchemists to despair (1967, 13: paragraph 203).

We are not accustomed to thinking of Mercurius as a killer or seducer — after all, he is the animating spirit of Alchemy and the messenger of the Gods. But Jung reminds us that he is Mercurius Duplex, and when not cast in his mediating role, he can be truly diabolical, the Black Magician. He is the "evil spirit ... imprisoned in the roots of the self" (1967, 13: paragraph 199). Represented as the dragon, the roaring fiery lion, the night raven, and the black eagle — all synonyms for the devil — Mercurius is a true malificus, and "like the devil, he also gets tricked" (Jung 1967, 13: 198). On his dark side, he is associated with the female serpent-daemon Lilith (Jung 1967, 13: paragraph 240) and with the dissolving spirit of Saturn which destroys everything (Jung 1967, 13: paragraph 227). As Jung says, "if Mercurius is not exactly the Evil One himself, he at least contains him (1967, 13: paragraph 228).[12]

The idea of an archetypal agency in the psyche attacking the ego from within stretches our usual Jungian notion of the compensatory nature of the unconscious and forces us to turn to object-relations theory — especially Ronald Fairbairn (1981) — for a better understanding. Fairbairn had another name for our diabolical Mercurius. He called him the "Internal Saboteur," and, like Freud, he emphasized the raw aggression of this figure. Fairbairn worked with children in Scotland who had been sexually molested during World War II. He was struck by the ironic fact that the more innocent and vulnerable the child, the more shame the child apparently felt for being assaulted. These children were never angry at their perpetrators, but instead saw them as loving and "good," taking all the anger and "badness" into themselves as self-directed hate and shame. The child's spontaneous aggression towards the "bad" abuser was inverted and taken in as an attack upon a "bad" self-representation by a persecutory Internal Saboteur.[13]

In this way, the child assured a "good" outer world at the price of a persecutory inner world, ruled by the Devil and his demons (diabolical Mercurius). According to Fairbairn, in the psychoanalytic situation, the goal must therefore be to help the patient take the risk of releasing his internalized "bad" objects so their libidinal cathexis can be resolved. "The resistance to this," says Fairbairn, "is the patient's constant temptation to exploit a `good' relationship with the analyst as a defence against taking this risk" (1981, 69). Fairborn wrote:

> I feel convinced [that] it is to the realm of these bad objects, rather than to the realm of the super-ego that the ultimate origin of all psychopathological developments is to be traced; for it may be said of all psychoneurotic and psychotic patients that, if a True Mass is being celebrated in the chancel, a Black Mass is being celebrated in the crypt. It becomes evident, accordingly, that the psychotherapist is the true successor to the exorcist, and that he is concerned, not only with "the forgiveness of sins," but also with "the casting out of devils" (1981, 70).

We are back, then, to Jung's earlier distinction between loss of soul and possession by a spirit. With the added insight of Fairbairn's analysis, we can see that the diabolical "spirit" that possesses Mary's inner world is both protective and persecutory. Each of these two aspects of the Mercurial self-care figure has an infantile ego-counterpart. On the one hand is the protective, smothering Mercurial "mother" of the lesser coniunctio, who seductively nurses a compliant, innocent, undemanding "good baby," feeding it on illusions and substitutes. This structure is "outpictured" in Mary's transference up to the moment of breakthrough. Mary is the good, innocent patient, and I am the idealized, caretaking "mother," nursing her on substitutes. On the other hand, Mary's inner world contains a violent, punishing, and diabolical Mercurial "mother," who tyranically represses a needy (therefore bad), enraged "baby," who is never allowed to show itself. Here, we have Mary and the zombie-serum injecting doctor. These two sides of the Mercurial self-care system are split apart and not allowed to know anything about each other. The reason for this split is to protect Mary from her deepest anxiety — the unspeakable terror she experienced when her infantile hatred of the abandoning mother threatened to utterly destroy the only dependable "world" she had.

At the crisis point in Mary's therapy outlined in our vignette, we could say that her internal, dependent, "bad" (because dependent) self-representation had just begun to be released from repression in the transference — her inner protector had begun to relinquish control. If Mary allows herself to feel her actual dependency on me (whom her self-care system cannot control — just as it could not control the unavailable mother), she simultaneously releases the potential rage and despair that she felt as a child and, with it, the incapacitating anxiety that accompanied the early trauma. Heretofore, she has only shown the "good," compliant, self-sufficient part. Now, she uncovers the "bad," needy, dependent part. This is very dangerous. If she uses the vacation phone number I gave her, she has to contend with the fact that — unlike her inner caretakers — I will often not be available. In other words, I will be "bad" just like her real mother, well-intentioned but flawed, and her rage will now come out at her therapist, who is no longer the ideal person she thought he was. Mary said to me during this period of the analysis: "If this is what we had to get to, why have you been so supportive and nice — how can I learn how to be bad if you're so good."[14]

Working Through, Mourning, and the Release of Mercurius

This was a critically important moment in Mary's therapy. She had always felt like she was "failing" in her analysis. Now, she intimates that someone might be failing her. We might think of this as Klein's depressive position, now organized in the transference — good and bad, love and hate experienced towards the same person. Without both love and aggression, the object is not "whole" or separate, and the self cannot be either. Without self-object separateness, there can be no mourning, and mourning is what heals the traumatized psyche. For Mary, this meant mourning her lost childhood, the lost mother she never had, and all the unlived life that her self-care system kept her from living. She had to suffer her own limitations, embracing her own unique tragic human life. Only this, shared now with another, could fill in the empty void in her stomach — that hollow cavern into which she kept pouring chocolate cake and ice cream. But trusting a real person meant betraying her inner daemon, and this meant sacrificing the only caretaking Guardian Angel/Demon she had ever trusted.[15] Of course, the betrayal of her daemon involved in this sacrifice is not really a betrayal because, in fact, it frees Mercurius for his real work to mediate the Greater Coniunctio.[16]

Setting Mercurius free to mediate, the Greater Coniunctio, can only happen after a wrestling match with the demonic side of our trickster-God. Symbolic work with these patients is not possible until we have met and fought with this destructive spirit, just like Jacob did with his dark angel at the river Jabok. And, like Jacob, we will probably be wounded in this battle. In any case, our full involvement will be required — personally and professionally — with love and hate, boundaries and space, intimacy and distance — in other words an active effort to hold the opposites. Often in this process, we must struggle with our own diabolical impulses, developing enough neutralized aggression to confront the Black Magician's seductiveness in the patient and in ourselves, while at the same time maintaining "rapport" with the patient's genuine woundedness and need. This struggle constitutes a genuine "moment of urgency" in the therapeutic process, and many treatments have been shipwrecked on either the Scylla of too much confrontation or the Charybdis of too much compassion and complicity with the undertow of the patient's malignant (Mercurial) regression.

And yet, we have all experienced in our work the utter freedom, joy, and aliveness that comes into our patients' lives and into the analytic work when the perilous passage between these twin dangers has been made and Mercurius is set free from his archetypal defensive functions to perform his true tasks as a psychopomp. Suddenly, the dreams start to cohere around a telos or direction. Suddenly, unconscious material starts to compensate the conscious ego attitude in a way which deepens the process immeasurably — just as Jung always said it did! Suddenly, the transference is freed of previously burdensome demands. The patient is filled with gratitude instead of bitterness and perhaps discovers a genuine religious attitude. Suddenly, the sessions are mutual and collaborative — often moving — and we are reminded why we do this extremely difficult work, and are reinspired to continue it.

These grace-like experiences are those in congress with the same shimmering God, whose diabolical shadow we have been wrestling with all along. Now, he turns his other face and blesses the patient and our efforts with a light that comes from all this darkness, like Lucifer's light, the *lumen naturae*, the light of nature itself. Here, Mercurius incarnates in the work as the God of revelation (Jung 1967, 13: paragraph 209), akin to the Holy Spirit, an *anima media natura* (the soul as intermediate nature) (Jung 1967, 13: paragraph 213), or, as the Alchemists describe him, a "life-giving power like a glue, holding the world together, standing in the middle between body and spirit" (Jung 1967, 13: paragraph 214). Here is the transcendent function, the capacity for imagination restored, the renewed possibility of a symbolic life.

We encounter here a supreme irony in our work with the psyche. The self-same powers that seemed so set on undermining our therapeutic efforts — so ostensibly devoted to death, dismemberment, and annihilation of consciousness — are the very reservoir from which new life, fuller integration, and true enlightenment derive. We come closer, here, to understanding the devil's self-description in Faust, when asked "Who are you then?" The devil responds:

> Part of that Power which would
> the Evil ever do, and ever does the Good (Faust 1941, 40).

Or, as Jung describes Mercurius: "[according to one view] he would be equal to one half of the Christian Godhead." He is, indeed, the dark chthonic half, but he is not simply evil as such, for he is called "good and evil," or a "system of the higher powers in the lower." He calls to mind that double figure which seems to stand behind both Christ and the devil — that enigmatic Lucifer whose attributes are shared by both (Jung 1967, 13: paragraph 223).

Conclusion

I think such a perverse figure in the psyche as the diabolical

Mercurius threatens our Jungian optimism about the "wisdom of the psyche" or the forward movement of the individuation process towards wholeness. For people like Mary, "wholeness" is a disaster because it means uniting her rage and love in one place, and this constellates disintegration anxiety! Instead, her demon seduces her into oneness, and we have seen the result — a "repetition compulsion" of self-destruction that leads not to soul-making, but to soul-breaking. This is genuine pathology, devoid of redemptive "meaning." We prefer not to think about genuine pathology in some branches of Jungian psychology. We would rather talk about the importance of "pathologizing" — its potential "meaning."

So, trauma patients like Mary force us to re-vision the "soul work" we do. They challenge our assumptions that if we just "stick with the image" and bring more imagination to the patient's problem, the splits will be healed. They challenge Jung's notion that individuation goes on in the unconscious whether the ego participates or not! In cases like Mary, we are working with the traumatic rupture in the capacity for imagination itself. The symbolic process is co-opted for defensive (self-cure) purposes and the dynamic opposition between the psyche's opposites, which is the basis of true symbolic life, is actively attacked and ruthlessly anesthetized by a diabolical "anti-mediating" factor, the underworld Mercurius. Under his supervision, all individuation comes to a halt. The psyche spins like the disengaged motor of a car, and life winds down into despair and eventual suicide.

In order to get this process moving again, we will have to engage the diabolical side of Mercurius at the self/world interface — in other words, in the transference, not just in the inner world. For Mary and me, the transference and countertransference were indispensable as tools for understanding. Indeed, she had no other intimate relationship in her life which she could "use" to "outpicture" her early traumatic abandonment and its accompanying annihilation anxiety. This is not always the case. I have seen some patients work through this level of primitive agony in relation to a close friend, a spouse, and, in one case, through a psychologically sensitive relationship to a beloved, yet injured, child. But when the patient is essentially alone in the world, the transference becomes the only relational container there is.

These formulations carry important implications for our discussion of trauma and "child abuse" in general. If my hypotheses are correct, this means that an archetypal, traumatogenic imago haunts these patient's psyches, partially confirming Jung's early proposition that:

> ... it now appears totally irrelevant whether the trauma really occurred or not. Experience shows us that fantasies can be just as traumatic in their effects as real traumata (1967, 4: paragraph 96).

This is very different from the popular notion in the current literature that these inner tormentors represent the "introjected" perpetrators of the literal abuse, in symbolic disguise. Writers like Judith Hermann (1992) or Lenore Terr (1990) follow this reductive line of reasoning, believing that, "trauma splits the psyche." Many contemporary psychotherapists, finding inner persecutory figures in their patients' dreams or fantasies, are inclined to the same literalistic fallacy — alleging incest or child abuse, as if a dream figure points only in the direction of outer reality. We know now that inner persecution by archetypal defensive figures is a common feature in the unconscious material of patients who have suffered unbearable (traumatic) anxiety. Such anxiety does accompany child abuse, but is also the result of many other factors, including parental neglect, external pressures on the parenting figure, and a lack of emotional fit between mother and baby. As Paul Kugler (1986) has pointed out in his excellent paper on Freud's "seduction theory," the concretistic tendency of modern psychological discourse leaves out the intermediate "imago" level which was central to both Freud's and Jung's understanding of the psyche.

Such concretism also leads to a facile politicization of the issue, with many people identifying with "innocent" (good) victims and blaming "responsible" (bad) perpetrators — when, in reality, every individual has both victim and perpetrator within. No doubt, actual child abuse, ritual cult abuse, and incest are much more common crimes against children than we ever thought possible, but there is also a sadistic, abusing agency in the psyche, and one that commits incest to boot! I hope I have shown that a deeper alchemical understanding of the psyche's archaic defenses demonstrates that trauma does not split the psyche —

instead, an inner psychological agency, occasioned by the traumatic anxiety, does the splitting. This does not make history irrelevant. It simply says that an inner agency is responsible for what happens psychologically after the traumatic anxiety has occurred.

Finally, if my analysis is correct, then one of the central concerns of the archetypal psyche is defense against unbearable anxiety. How can Jung have overlooked this? The answer to this question is complicated, but I believe that in his zeal to elaborate a model of the psyche that was generative — not based on drive and defense — Jung moved too far away from Freud's pessimistic pathologizing into an optimism about the psyche which was equally one-sided.

For example, when Jung and Freud were still together and immersed in exploration of incest fantasies, Jung was always inclined to ask, "what was the purpose of these fantasies?" and "why the mythic parallels?" What looked to Freud like a paradisal longing for the mother had a larger meaning, a "telos" or direction, and was to be understood as the psyche's instinctive desire to dissolve the ego's present conflict in more archaic layers of the unconscious in order to be reborn anew. This was Jung's explanation for incest-symbolism. The traumatized ego regresses because it seeks to be healed by inclusion in something larger — not just because it wants to escape a conflict or make itself feel better.

In other words, Jung tended to see these unconscious fantasies as "meaningful" efforts on the part of the whole psyche to heal the split personal ego by immersing it in transpersonal energies — dissolving it, as it were, in a mythic structure and narrative when the personal, historical structure, and narrative had broken down (in the language of Alchemy, dissolve and coagulate).

My analysis suggests that Jung was on the right track, but that for the traumatized psyche, the "meaning" is in a different place. "Meaningful efforts" are being made by the psyche, but these included unconscious efforts to destroy meaning! Mercurius cannot perform his "meaningful" mediating function if there has been severe trauma. His function then becomes a perverse, repetitious, attack on meaning in order to dissolve the traumatically fractured ego in the oblivion of dismembered illusion. This is a defense just as Freud claimed — but it is an archetypal defense engineered by the Self in the interest (telos) of the personality's survival — even though the surviving ego may become a zombie, without meaning. So, if we apply Jung's own teleological analysis to the very defensive processes he tended to overlook, we discover a transcendent meaning that satisfies us — even though it is not quite the same optimistic meaning that Jung saw as he tried to differentiate his position from Freud's, back in 1913, more than eight decades ago.

Notes

[1] For example, in *Mysterium*, Jung said:

> ... the view that good and evil are spiritual forces outside us, and that man is caught in the conflict between them, is more bearable by far than the insight that the opposites are the ineradicable and indispensable preconditions of all psychic life, so much so that life itself is guilt (1967, 14: 170).

[2] Jung, apparently, also kept his distance clinically. For example, von Franz reports that Jung supervised her first clinical case — an animus-possessed woman who was extremely irritating. Jung saw the woman for a consultation and the next day told von Franz: "kick that lady out of analysis, and tell her what a cheating, lying devil she was" (von Franz 1974, 172, 195).

[3] Especially the affair with Sabina Spielrein, who, interestingly, thereafter was preoccupied with the issue of destruction and whose paper, "Destruction as a Cause of Coming Into Being," may have been a source for Freud's idea of the Death Instinct. For further discussion of this possibility, see Kerr (1988).

[4] For a discussion of how addictive submission substitutes for the deeper craving to surrender, see Ghent (1990, 108-35).

[5] Julia Kristeva (1989), the French linguist and Lacanian psychoanalyst, articulates this problem in an interesting way. She uses the image of the Black Sun to indicate a strong, powerful — even numinous — "presence" in the unconscious of depressed patients. (We might think of it as the negative side of the Self — as represented by Mercurius, a kind of negative numinosum.) This inner presence, Kristeva says, is really an Absence, a "light without representation," a sadness which is "the most archaic expression of an unsymbolizable unnameable narcissistic wound which becomes the depressed person's sole object of attachment ... an

object they tame and cherish for lack of another" (1989, 13). She calls this non-object, "The Thing." Describing patients very much like Mary, Kristeva says:

> ... [all symbolic] language starts with [entails] a negation [transcendence] *(Verneinung)* of loss, along with the depression occasioned by mourning. "I have lost an essential object ... (my mother)" is what the speaking seems to be saying. "But no, I have found her again in signs, or rather, since I consent to lose her, I have not lost her (that is the negation), I can recover her in language" (Kristeva 1989, 43).

Depressed persons, on the contrary, disavow the negation: they cancel it out, suspend it, and nostalgically fall back on the real object of their loss (what Kristeva calls "The Thing" — the "non-lost object." The denial *(Verlegnung)* of negation would thus be the exercise of an impossible mourning, the setting up of a fundamental sadness and an artificial, unbelievable language, cut out of the painful background that is not accessible to any signifier (1989, 43-44). The result is that traumatic memories are not repressed, but constantly evoked as the denial of negation prevents the work of repression (Kristeva 1989, 46) and symbol-formation, which depends upon the psyche's creative elaboration.

6 For this distinction, I am indebted to R. van Loben Sels (personal communications, 1993)

7 See Shengold 1989 for a discussion of how severely traumatized patients utilize autohypnosis as a defense against unbearable anxiety.

8 Sandor Ferenczi (1988), especially, emphasizes the fact that our inner figure is not just a persecutory demon, but also a guardian angel, namely, duplex. He reports his treatment of a young woman who had a history of violent and repeated sexual abuse by her father from infancy. Her dreams and fantasies showed three inner figures — one a stuperous infant who was completely helpless and who only wanted to die, an older child who carried the abuse memories and abreacted them in therapy, and then a kind of transpersonal entity Ferenczi called "Orpha." Representing the "organizing life instincts," Orpha was both protector and persecutor. At times of unbearable trauma, it was up to Orpha to arrange for the patient's suicide. If this proved to be impossible because of hospitalization, then, in place of death, Orpha chopped up the personality, dispersing it into fragments — thereby driving it insane in order to prevent death.

[9] Readers familiar with James Masterson's (1976) useful approach to the borderline patient will recognize in this description his Rewarding Object Relations Part Unit (RORU) — corresponding to the self-soothing nature of Mercurius' relation to the "good," self-sufficient, infantile part — and his Withdrawing Object Relations Part Unit (WORU) — corresponding to the cold, attacking aspect of Mercurius' relation to the "bad," dependent, infantile part.

[10] Of course, one could argue that the evil doctor in the zombie hospital is an image of me in the transference. Some analysts might say that Mary unconsciously experienced my offer of the phone number as a trick, colluding with her own defenses and, therefore, her dream represented me as diabolical — delivering de-humanizing serum. This interpretation cannot be discarded out of hand. The dangers of collusion with the False-self patient are very real. As I already suggested, to the extent that I was trying to "help" Mary not to feel the full impact of her despair and anxiety during previous years of her therapy, I would have been in collusion with the diabolical side of Mercurius. In this way, Mercurius shows us the diabolical underside of our therapeutic good intentions — always present to seduce the therapist, as well as the patient, out of the work of analysis. Such seduction is a special danger when the Black Magician appears in the context of an eroticized transference.

Alternatively, from a classical Freudian slant, one could interpret the injecting doctor sexually, that is, underneath my "nice exterior" in the transference I was envisioned by Mary's dream as planning to inject her with my penis and turn her into a zombie. Neither of these interpretations is "wrong." Each is just too facile and too reductive, translating the dream image back into the concrete reality of the analyst from its "disguised" form in the unconscious, as though the unconscious were preoccupied only with the transference. If we stay with the image, we notice that the evil doctor and Mary's food demon seem to share the same "intention." Both seduce her out of "her world" into "their world," where she ends up in an altered state, "spaced out" or "a zombie." These are basically non-feeling states. So our diabolical figure's "purpose" seems to be to get her into a "numb," depersonalized state. Why would he do this? In keeping with my analysis, it would be in order to prevent Mary's ego from experiencing what he envisioned as a threat to her "sanity," namely a real relationship in which she might begin to trust again, only to be massacred. He would massacre her first in the inner world.

11 This idea is taken over from Bion by James Grotstein, who elaborates it at some length, also describing a personified psychic agency that carries out these attacks. An attack on linking, Grotstein says,

> ... results in attacks on the capacity to link thoughts and perceptions ... different components of the perceptual, cognitive, and affective systems may be severed. This attack on links amounts to rendering experience inconsequential; the significance of facts for truth undergoes eclipse or extinction (1981, 92-93).

Elsewhere, Grotstein (1987, 317-19) describes how, in his work with chronically depressed or addicted patients, a diabolical "alien self" — a virtual "living phantom" — seemed to hold a more dependent, helpless self "hostage within its powerful snare" and fought for its own autonomous destiny.

12 Jung's interest in Mercurius was precisely because this duplex God contained within himself both evil and good, and thereby represented the nature of psychic reality more faithfully than the split dualism of Christianity, where the opposites have come apart as Christ and the Devil.

13 Ferenczi (1955) makes essentially the same point, saying that the traumatized child, unable to protest abuse, identifies himself with the aggressor, thus maintaining feelings of tenderness towards the outer persecutor, while now menaced by an internal (introjected) one.

14 Mary's point was well taken here, yet her defenses needed me to remain the "good" world/mother until she could "own" some of her real (bad) dependency. A further implication of Fairbairn's analysis for our case is that her protector/persecutor embodies all the aggression that always eludes Mary's pale ingratiating ego. This aggression is not available to her for adaptation in the world, or for differentiation of herself from others, or to help her express herself. It is all tied up in this inverted form. Confronting this figure, then, and working with him both in the transference and in active imagination, can help liberate aggression in the service of the ego and of adaptation.

15 We should remember that the word "sacrifice" means "to make

sacred," and that Jung saw it as a crucial stage in the individuation process. Viewed through the lens of our current discussion, sacrifice is a simultaneous killing of a "God" and an innocent "baby" in its care — in other words of the archetypal self-care system — in the service of opening us to the world. Giving up the self-care system has never been easy. Its sacrifice has been a major problem in the development of humanity's ability to trust relationship to otherness, both outer and inner. Apparently, when the soul has been murdered, (Shengold) it cannot be restored without a further (ritual) murder of the quasi-delusional, self-care structures that insulate the ego from reality.

[16] In this connection, it is interesting that Jung is at a loss to explain why Mercurius is trapped in a bottle in the early part of the Grimms Fairy Tale he uses in his famous essay, "The Spirit Mercurius" (1967, 13: paragraphs 191-250). This, and the fact that a boy frees him, Jung says, "must be described as alchemically incorrect ... [because the alchemists] wanted to keep him in the bottle in order to transform him ... " (1967, 13: paragraph 203). According to our current analysis, Mercurius must be released from his service to archetypal defensive processes (where his energies are self-attacking and negating), in order to engage in the transformative processes of individuation. But this release does not happen automatically. It must happen relationally with another person first.

Bibliography

Balint, Michael. 1979. *The Basic Fault: Therapeutic Aspects of Regression*. Evanston: Northwestern Universities Press.

Edinger, Edward F. 1985. *The Anatomy of the Psyche: Alchemical Symbolism in Psychotheraphy*. LaSalle, Illinois: Open Court.

Estes, Clarisa Pinkola. 1992. *Women Who Run With The Wolves*. New York: Ballantine Books.

Fairbairn, Ronald W.D. 1981. *Psychoanalytic Studies of the Personality*. London: Routledge & Kegan Paul.

Ferenczi, Sandor. 1955. "Confusion of Tongues between Adults and the Child." In *Final Contributions to the Problems and Methods of Psychoanalysis*, edited by Michael Balint, 156-67. New York: Brunner/Mazel.

———. 1988. *Clinical Diary*. Cambridge: Harvard University Press.

Fordham, Michael. 1974. "Defences of the Self." *Journal of Analytical Psychology* 19, no. 2: 192-99.

von Franz, Marie Louise. 1974. *Shadow and Evil in Fairy Tales.* Zurich: Spring Publications.

Freud, Sigmund. [1923] 1973a. "Ego & Id." *Standard Edition of the Complete Psychological Works of Sigmund Freud* 19. London: Hogarth Press.

——. [1920] 1973b. "New Introductory Lectures." *Standard Edition of the Complete Psychological Works of Sigmund Freud* 22. London: Hogarth Press.

Ghent, E. 1990. "Masochism, Submission, Surrender." *Contemporary Psychoanalysis* 26, no. 1: 108-35.

Goethe, Johann Wolfgang von. 1941. *Faust,* translated by G. M. Priest. New York: Knopf.

Grotstein, James S. 1981. *Splitting and Projective Identification.* New York: Jason Aronson, Inc.

——. 1987. "An Object-relations Perspective on Resistance in Narcissistic Patients." In *Techniques of Working with Resistance.* New York: Jacob Aronson Inc.

Herman, Judith. 1992. *Trauma and Recovery.* New York: Basic Books.

Jung, C.G. 1947. "Wotan." In *Essays on Contemporary Events,* translated by Barbara Hannah, 1-16. London: Kegan Paul.

——. 1961. *Memories, Dreams, Reflections,* edited by Amiela Jaffe. New York: Vintage Books.

——. 1967. "The Spirit of Mercurius." In *Alchemical Studies. Collected Works* 13. Princeton: Princeton University Press for the Bollingen Foundation.

Kerr, John. 1988. "Beyond the Pleasure Principle and Back Again." In *Freud, Appraisals and Reappraisals: Contributions to Freud Studies,* edited by Paul Stepansky, 3: 3-80. New Jersey: Analytic Press.

Kohut, Heinz. 1984. *How Does Analysis Cure,* edited by Arnold Goldberg and Paul Stepansky. Chicago: University of Chicago Press.

Khan, Masud R. 1974. "Towards an Epistemology of Cure." In *The Privacy of the Self,* edited by Khan, 93-98. New York: International Universities Press, Inc.

Kristeva, Julia. 1989. *Black Sun: Depression and Melancholia.* New York:

Columbia University Press.

Kugler, Paul. 1986. "Childhood Seduction: Physical and Emotional." *Spring*, 40-60.

Leonard, L.S. 1990. *Witness to the Fire: Creativity and the Veil of Addiction.* Boston: Shambhala.

——. 1993. *Meeting the Madwoman: An Inner Challenge for Feminine Spirit.* New York: Bantam Books.

van Loben Sels, Robin. 1993. "Dreams as Daily Bread." Temenos Institute, Westport Connecticut.

Masterson, James. 1976. *Psychotherapy of the Borderline Adult.* New York: Brunner/Mazel.

Murray, J.A.H., ed. 1897. *New English Dictionary.* Oxford.

Shengold, Lawrence. 1989. *Soul Murder: The Effects of Childhood Abuse and Deprivation.* New York: Fawcett Columbine.

Stein, Leopold. 1967. "Introducing Not-Self." *Journal of Analytical Psychology* 12, no. 2: 97-113.

Terr, Lenore. 1990. *Too Scared to Cry: Psychic Trauma in Childhood.* New York: Harper & Row.

Winnicott, D. W. 1971. "The Location of Cultural Experience." In *Playing and Reality,* edited by Winnicott, 95-103. New York: Basic Books, Inc.

——. 1989. "Fear of Breakdown." In *Psychoanalytic Explorations,* edited by Clare Winnicott, 87-95. Cambridge, Massachusetts: Harvard University Press.

Chapter 6

Seduction, Psychotherapy, and the Alchemical *Glutinum Mundi*

Lionel Corbett

Introduction

This essay suggests a possible amplification of the alchemical concept of the *glutinum mundi,* or the glue of the world. This notion is not mentioned much in the the Jungian literature, but I think it contains the germ of an idea that casts some light on the dynamics of relationships and that is also relevant to the therapeutic process. I also believe that this idea helps us to understand more about the need to seduce, and how this may operate in psychotherapy.

Relationships: Mixing Psyches and Sticking Them Together

The Jungian literature on alchemy has always emphasized the subjective state of mind of the alchemist, as though he were somehow isolated from the effects of other minds; in other words, when discussing what he saw in his laboratory, we have neglected to take into account the influence of the alchemist's relationships. Surely, the alchemist's preoccupation with the mingling of elements reveals projections which had to do not only with his own intrapsychic material, but also with his experience of the mingling of psyches — his own with others — as this affected his search for the Self. This search is not carried out or consummated in isolation; it cannot be completed without relationships. The frequent references to the alchemist's *soror mystica* are usually dismissed as if she were only a laboratory assistant, but perhaps the contents of their alembics were sometimes a function of what was happening between the two of them, rather than only a reflection of the alchemist's solipsistic preoccupations.

Alchemy quintessentially involved the mixing of elements, since the alchemists knew that significant change would otherwise be interminably slow. And the same is true of people; change is more likely to occur in the context of an important relationship than when we are unrelated, which is sometimes why people stay unrelated. Mixing two psyches is rather like mixing two elements, in the sense that surprises emerge. For example, oxygen and hydrogen are dry gasses; when combined, they produce the surpising new quality of wetness that is hard to predict from the properties of the individual elements. So it can be when we mix psyches; when we meet certain people, we sense the potential for some unknown, new, and sometimes inaccessible quality that could emerge from the combination of the two of us. We feel an urge to be with the other in order to discover what this new thing may be which is forming within us. The new possibility is sensed as an internal pressure which arises from the unconscious, where the mixing has already begun. Consciously, we are only aware of a diffuse excitement; we know that something has stirred us, but we do not know what it will look like. We only know that we must have it, and sometimes it seems as if we can only get it from one particular person. I believe that when this gripping or drawing together occurs, a type of intrapsychic "glue" has begun to activate and become sticky; eventually it will set, forming a bond of varying degrees of strength and flexibility.

Why is all of this necessary? What is the difference between the self alone and the individual in relationship, such that there is such a powerful motivation for us to be in relationship? I believe that the alchemists were alluding to this mystery when they described the *glutinum mundi* as the transforming substance which acts as a life force, uniting soul and body (Jung 1968, 12: paragraph 209). What, then, is the nature of this glue which holds us and relationships together and which allows people in relationships to be held together? The search for this glue seems to be a fundamental human urge, which I want to address particularly from the vantage point of its manifestations within psychotherapy. I believe that one of the unconscious reasons people seek therapy is to find this glue, this mysterious bonding agent which will hold us together when we feel tenuous and fragile. For many people, the possession of this glue is more important than the usual sacred cows of insight or of making the unconscious conscious, neither of which necessarily perform this function, and both of which may occur in the analytic process with no real structural change in the personality. As well, I suggest that what motivates a good deal of sexual behavior and seductiveness, both within and without of therapy, is not simply the desire for genital sexuality, but, at a deeper level, is actually the need for this glue.

Here, of course, I differ from Freud, and I am in the camp of the psychoanalytic self-psychologists because I do not believe that sexuality itself is always the bedrock motive even when we are actually having sex. Overtly sexual relationships are often being driven by something deeper, more fundamental. This has to do with the need to be held together as a cohesive personality, so that we do not easily fall apart with unbearable anxiety or depression, so that we can maintain reasonable self esteem, and so that we can withstand the usual fluctuations of life's successes and failures with reasonable equanimity, without excessive inflation or despair. I believe that the elusive bonding agent which is required here is what the alchemists referred to as the *glutinum mundi*. Where I am definitively Jungian, here, is my belief that this mysterious compound is a "secretion" of the Self. It is secreted maximally between people; the Self influences the field in which we live, as it were "magnetically" drawing people to us to provide certain experiences. This glue is an important component of the attraction which we have for others and which they have for us. In therapy, when the Self is constellated within the therapeutic relationship, the glue flows freely. This glue is, I believe, the psychological matrix which allows the *coniunctio* to develop.

In their ideas of the *glutinum mundi* and the *coniunctio*, the alchemists intuited something archetypally that took several hundred years for psychoanalytic psychology to articulate at the personal level. But this has finally been done, with the result that we can now at least describe the function of the glue, if not its essential nature, at the personalistic level. The psychoanalytic self-psychologists describe this function as the selfobject experience; in its archetypal form, it is described in Jung's essay on the transference where it is known as the *coniunctio*. If we merge the archetypal and personal levels, it seems that the glue represents the unfolding of the Self within human relationships in such a way that the participants feel joined to each other. The selfobject experience allows the repair of elements of the self that need strengthening or rebuilding.

The Selfobject Experience

First, let me emphasize that I use the term "selfobject," as it is described by Heinz Kohut (1971, 1977, 1984), whose usage is embedded in a different theoretical framework than the usage by Michael Fordham (1976, 20-21; 1985, 20), which is an object relations theory approach. Although these writers use the same term, they refer to totally different subjective experiences which bear little resemblance to each other.[1]

In psychoanalytic self-psychology, the term "selfobject" is used to refer to the subjective or intrapsychic experience of another person (not the person herself) who is necessary for the maintenance of the cohesion, vitality, or integrity of the self — anyone, that is, who keeps us feeling glued together and enhances our sense of well-being. Kohut (1984, 47) believed that the need for such a relationship begins in infancy and never goes away, but gradually matures — he objected to Mahler's postulate of separation as the goal of development. Within his thought, the need for sustaining others is lifelong. This is a different value system than the patriarchal autonomy-independence morality of Freud.

Our selfobject needs are thought to be:

(1) Mirror needs, which include such needs as those for affirmation and confirmation of our value; for emotional attunement and resonance; to be the gleam in somebody's eye; to be approved of, seen, wanted, appreciated, and accepted. Here, the developmental necessity is to transform healthy infantile grandiosity and exhibitionism into mature adult self-esteem, normal levels of ambition, pride in performance, and an inner sense of one's own worth.

(2) Idealization needs, such as the need for an alliance with, or to be psychologically a part of, a figure who carries high status and importance — who is respected, admired, wise, protective, and strong, and, hence, can be a source of soothing when I feel that I myself do not possess these qualities. Such a figure is both calming and inspiring, and the intrapsychic experience of merger with the selfobject lends us the strength to maintain ourselves when we feel frightened, or it gives us direction when we are in search

of meaning and goals. Eventually, as this line of development matures, it leads to an inner sense of direction and to internally derived goals and values.

(3) Twinship or alter-ego needs, which involve the need for sameness based on similarity of abilities, requiring the sense of being understood by someone "like me." To be in a community of people of shared values and beliefs or to have the quietly sustaining presence of one such person is supporting and enhancing to the self.

(4) There is sometimes a need for a benign adversary, an opposing force who allows active opposition, which confirms one's autonomy, at the same time as that person continues to be supportive and responsive. The adversarial selfobject (Wolf 1988) allows assertiveness without the loss of the other.

(5) Efficacy needs allow us to feel that we can have an effect on the other person and that we are able to evoke what we need from him: "If I can elicit a response, I must be somebody."

All of this emphasis on our ineradicable connection to others moves psychotherapy out of what R.D. Stolorow and G.E. Atwood (1992) call the "myth of the isolated mind." Classical Jungian analysis, with its emphasis on introspectively obtained data from dreams and active imagination, has often been guilty of this attitude. In fact, we are always selves in a matrix of other selves, or selfobjects, who are responsive to our needs to varying degrees, in ways that sustain us or glue us together; we are never selves in a psychological vacuum. Intrapsychically, the self, like the Self, does not end at the skin. It includes those who are important to us, and some of the content of our intrapsychic imagery is accordingly tied to the vicissitudes of these relationships. In Jung's words: "In the deepest sense we all dream not out of ourselves but out of what lies between us and the other" (1973, 172).

Selfobject experiences are subjective functions; intrapsychically and often unconsciously, the other is acting as a part of the self, carrying out functions that the self cannot provide for itself, and, in this way, acting as a psychological extension of the self. Thus, selfobject needs are like glue for the developing personality. In infancy, qualities of the child's self, such as its structural integrity and vitality, are determined by the qualities of his selfobject relationships as they have been transmutingly internalized

(Kohut 1971). To the extent that the selfobject milieu is healthy, the self develops with cohesion and resilience; to the extent that the milieu is unresponsive to the child's unfolding needs, the self develops varying degrees of structural deficit and proneness to fragmentation. When the child's selfobject needs are unmet, they remain active but immature; there is then a lifelong need to find someone to supply them. The mirror hungry or idealization hungry personality lacks the internal glue which would make him feel put together and so constantly searches for it externally, by means of a relationship or situation which will provide what is missing.

In the therapeutic situation, the original childhood need resurfaces; in fact, it is often the underlying motive for seeking therapy. If it is then responded to properly, the deficit in the self can potentially be healed because the selfobject experience is internalized in the context of the relationship with the therapist. When this is established and the glue is bonding, the patient feels alive and integrated; when it is disrupted, for example by separation or because of the therapist's traumatic behavior, the patient feels fragmented and devitalized. (Discussion of the details of the process by which this occurs would take us too far from our subject.) It is important to note that the process of meeting selfobject needs can be carried out by the therapist in an automatic, intuitive, or even unconscious manner, and is often considered to be a non-specific aspect of the therapeutic process, such as the "therapeutic alliance." In such cases, the therapist may attribute the success of the therapy to other factors (depending on his or her theoretical orientation) which, in fact, are peripheral. For example, in the case of Jungian therapists, careful attention to the patient's dreams and active imagination may sometimes be helpful because they provide a vehicle for the selfobject process, while the content of the interpretation may be of secondary importance.

A Jungian Contribution: The Archetypal Basis of the Selfobject Relationship

I suggest that the unfolding of selfobject needs, whether for the first time in childhood or as they are repeated within the therapeutic setting, actually represent the unfolding of archetypal elements of the Self. It is a cliché by now to repeat that the Self is the archetypal basis of the ego, but it has never been very clear in what way the Self acts as such a blueprint. Selfobject needs seem to be aspects of the Self which unfold according to an inner ground plan, and which require environmental responses for them to be humanized and integrated into the structures of a personal self — or, to allow the Self to incarnate into a self. (They are deintegrates in Fordham's sense.) To the extent that these elements are well dealt with, they form part of the structures of positive complexes; selfobject failure helps form negative complexes. In therapy, we are called upon to perform selfobject functions which the patient cannot provide for himself because they have never been built into his self structures. Thus, at first it takes both participants for him to experience a whole sense of self. The intense, but unrecognized, numinosity of these needs occurs because they are aspects of the Self which have been constellated as part of the developing *coniunctio;* selfobject needs are the personally felt elements of this archetypal manifestation.

Depiction of the Coniunctio and Selfobject Needs in the Rosarium

The central image in Jung's (1966) discussion of the transference is that of the *coniunctio,* which he believes symbolizes a process of the union of opposites, initially in the unconscious. Jung suggests that this image represents the archetypal basis of the transference. To illustrate his point, he uses the *Rosarium Philosophorum,* a series of alchemical woodcuts which depict male and female figures in various stages of relationship, or of intrapsychic mingling. In therapy, the relationship between therapist and patient is a reflection of, or an externalization of, two intrapsychic worlds as they interact to gradually develop such a condition in which the two psyches merge or join. This process is helpful for several reasons. It allows previously unmanageable material to be integrated, missing structures to form, and the safe experience of the Self. It is the experience of the Self within the therapeutic field that accounts for the latter's numinosity. The Self must include within it the psyches of both participants since the Self is the totality of consciousness. Thus, both participants are immersed within a shared intersubjective field whose nature is determined by the Self. Since the Self always tends towards individuation, the particular material which is constellated within the field will be specific for the needs and difficuties of both therapist and patient. This means that the patient may act as a selfobject for the therapist, often unconsciously, and the therapist can be expected, in Kohut's phrase, to be "engaged in depth."

None of this is particularly controversial, but there is a need to depart from Jung in one important way, namely his insistence on the importance of defining the *coniunctio* only in terms of the union of opposites. Many post-Jungian writers have questioned Jung's idea that the psyche is necessarily structured in terms of opposites. For example, A. Samuels (1985) points out that such a perception of psychic functioning ignores the mutual support, complementarity, gradual change, and subtle transitions which are also found within the psyche. Instead of insisting on an oppositional psychology, I suggest that the "chymical marriage," or the supreme act of union which depicted the consummation of the alchemical opus (Jung 1970, 14: paragraph 104), does not so much consist of the union of opposite qualities, but is achieved by joining with whatever is missing from oneself in order to feel whole or to repair developmental damage. This may be more of some quality which we already have, such as masculinity or femininity, or it may be that we need a quality such as fathering or mothering which can only be provided by an older man or woman. Often, however, the necessary factor may be something that everyone needs, such as a particular selfobject function, which can be provided by a relationship with either a man or a woman, as long as that person is able to provide specifically what is needed for the ongoing growth of the personality. All of this has obvious implications for the choice of a therapist of a particular gender.

In the presence of an established selfobject relationship, we feel alive and cohesive. In other words, within this domain, it takes two people to experience one whole sense of self. This idea is expressed in the *Rosarium* pictures of two-ness, which is at the same time one-ness. The heads of the figures are not joined because the merger is not felt cognitively. But the felt sense is that the self is maintained as long as our relationship is intact. The urge to form such a union occurs because of a feeling of something missing in myself. In its attempt to restore or provide this quality, the Self extends an aspect of itself into the environment in the form of a selfobject need for another person; when this is responded to, the self is supported. The *Rosarium* woodcuts depict various stages of this process of union for the sake of completion.

For example, Figure 1, entitled "The King and Queen" (Jung 1966, 16: 213) illustrates the initial stage of the relationship, still at the persona stage. Figure 2, "Immersion in the Bath" (Jung 1966, 16: 243) indicates the shared psychological space in which the participants find themselves. It depicts what Kohut (1971) calls "prolonged empathic immersion" in the patient's inner world, here at a stage before any internal bonding has occured. Figure 3, "The Conjunction" (Jung 1966, 16: 249) on the surface looks like an erotic encounter, but actually represents an initial attraction based on selfobject needs that are so intense that they feel sexual. These needs are still unconscious, which is why the scene is depicted under water. As we shall see, this sexualization of selfobject needs is a very important mechanism; the overt sexuality covers the presense of deeper needs for affirmation or idealization.

Figure 4, entitled "Death" (Jung 1966, 16: 259), begins the series of images with two heads and one body. Jung (1966, 16: paragraph 467) believes that it represents both the *putrefactio* and the *conceptio* at the same time. This stage is, therefore, likened to a grain of wheat buried in the earth, which dies to allow new life. It represents the loss of individual selfhood in the service of the development of a new self out of the decay of old structures. Because it begins the seed of the selfobject experience laid down in the unconscious, it is also a *germinatio*. Figure 5, "Ascent of the Soul" (Jung 1966, 16: 269), which Jung describes as a "dark state of disorientation" (1966, 16: paragraph 476), represents those states of soul loss that occur as a result of disruption of the self-selfobject bond, leading to despair and confusion in the relationship. It is noteworthy that the alchemists described the existence of a "universal solvent," as well as the *glutinum*; this solvent may refer to the sense that one is falling apart as a result of the loss of the tie to an important selfobject. Figure 6, the "Purification" (Jung 1966, 16: 275), which depicts falling dew from heaven, and Figure 7 or the "Return of the Soul" (Jung 1966, 16: 285) represent the healing of this disruption and the reanimation of the relation-

ship. Figure 8, "The Rebis" (Jung 1966, 16: 307), which Jung calls
the new birth, depicts the full development of the selfobject tie, or
selfhood, in the presence of an established relationship with the
other.

Within the alchemical metaphor, this stage is technically a
"lesser" *coniunctio* since the self at this stage still needs further,
more conscious, differentiation. This is found in Figure 9, "The
Risen Christ," the final figure of the series, which Jung did not use
in his essay, representing the risen Christ. I take this image to
mean that the Self can finally become an internal experience for
the self. This state of mind is a product of mature selfhood, at
which time other selves are seen to be simply other fragments of
the Self, not essentially separate from one's own self. The original
Self of childhood, with which contact had been lost for a long
time, is resurrected, but now as a conscious experience. It is then
as if the philosopher's stone is finally created within the personality.

Here, I should note that Nathan Schwartz-Salant (1984, 1989)
has interpreted the *Rosarium* woodcuts in terms of projective
identification, assuming that they represent states of the inner
couple which are found in all relationshops. He also finds that
difficulties in the *coniunctio-nigrido* sequence dominates work
with borderline personalities. His work is seminal in the area of
the translation of archetypal imagery into categories which can be
discussed within the framework of personalistic psychoanalytic
theory. However, I differ from his interpretation of the *Rosarium*.
Primarily, I agree with those authors (Stolorow, Brandschaft and
Atwood 1987; Stolorow and Atwood 1992) who question the justification for some of the assumptions implicit in the very concept
of projective identification. However, I do lean on Schwartz-
Salant's idea that sexual acting out is often the result of a blun-
dering search for the experience of the *coniunctio,* here conceptu-
alized in terms of selfobject theory rather than Kleinian theory.

The Erotic in Psychotherapy: Seduction as the Search for the Glutinum Mundi

In this section, I hope to clarify something of the function of sexuality in psychotherapy, with the assumption that sexual acting out
is often due to a gross misunderstanding of the purpose of an

Figure 1: The King and Queen

Source: Jung (1966, 16: 213)

Figure 2: Immersion in the Bath

Source: Jung (1966, 16: 243)

Figure 3: The Conjunction

Source: Jung (1966, 16: 249)

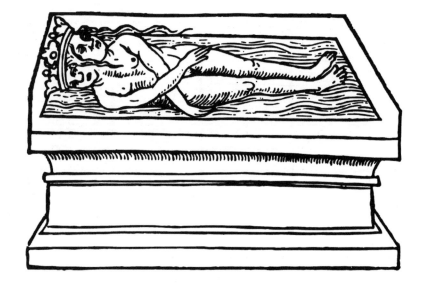

Figure 4: Death

Source: Jung (1966, 16: 259)

Figure 5: Ascent of the Soul

Source: Jung (1966, 16: 269)

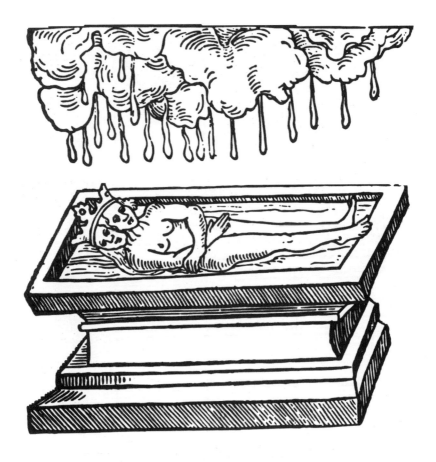

Figure 6: Purification

Source: Jung (1966, 16: 275)

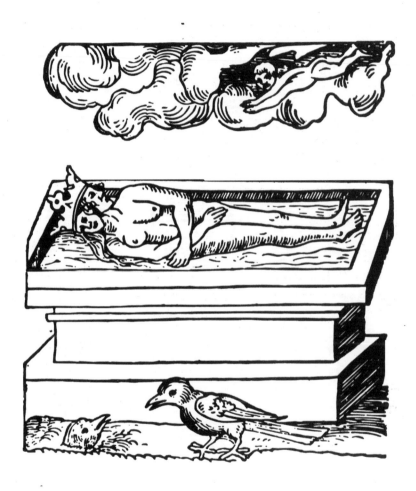

Figure 7: Return of the Soul

Source: Jung (1966, 16: 285)

Figure 8: The Rebis

Source: Jung (1966, 16: 307)

Figure 9: The Risen Christ

Source: McLean (1980)

erotic therapeutic field. I believe that what is sometimes attributed exclusively to countertransference acting out may also occur because of simple ignorance of the fact that the patient's selfobject needs may become sexualized. Greater understanding of this dimension of our own, and of the patient's, sexuality as it manifests within therapy, will prevent the therapist from repeating the traumatic, pathogenic behavior of the patient's early caregivers. In the face of the demands made by the child's needs, his early selfobjects either acted out disastrously, or defensively collapsed or retaliated. The therapeutic response to such demands must be very different.

My major point in this section is one which is often made by psychoanalytic self-psychologists, namely that sexuality has more than one meaning, and can only be understood in the context of the overall state of the self. Sexuality can enrich a cohesive self, or it can be used to bolster or hold together an enfeebled self which is in danger of falling apart. The latter situation must not be confused with a simple desire for genital sexuality; in such cases, sexuality is used to meet selfobject, or gluing, functions. If we look at the functions of sexuality in the service of maintaining the self, we see that it can do so in many ways. Sexuality is used to enhance self-esteem by allowing us to be admired and wanted. It allows us to feel powerful and in control. Sexuality involves being valued and responded to, being special in someone's eyes — feeling wanted, desirable, and seen. We can be a part of an admired person by whom we are held and soothed, or contained emotionally, at the same time as we are free to let go of inhibitions. We can use sexuality to avoid being lonely; to organize or control a relationship; to be stimulated when we are depressed, bored, or empty; or to become revitalized when apathetic.

To illustrate these mechanisms in practice, consider the individual who feels desperately anxious, lonely, or depressed, so that they go to to a bar to pick up or seduce someone — almost anyone — to alleviate their painful emptiness. The sex which results comes about because of a desperate need for a selfobject; it is not simply the result of a need for sex. Such a person wants to be held, soothed, contained, and cared for in order to prevent fragmentation; they are not merely seeking relief of a drive or dealing with an Oedipal difficulty, as classical Freudian theory might hold.

Simply stated, they are trying to find someone who will help them feel better. This example illustrates the fact that sexuality is not just about sex; raw sexuality of this kind, as Kohut puts it, is a disintegration product seen when the self falls apart.

Such a scenario reveals a misconception found within both classical Freudian theory and object relations theory; for many people with a relatively tenuous sense of self, there is no such thing as an important person who is, at the same time, a totally separate object in the simple traditional sense. If we look at the evolution of the idea of the function of the object, or of relationships within dynamic psychology, we see a spectrum that begins with classical theory in which personal desire is primary, but not its relational context. Other people are mostly important inasmuch as they allow us to discharge the drives, and the intensity of the drives explains attachment. Later, in British Object Relations theory, the drives themselves gradually became less primary, and relationships became important; the drive became a way of relating, and there even emerged the idea of a drive to relationship. Eventually, for some Object Relations theorists, sexuality and aggression became derivative; people need relationship at all cost. (In the first case, relationship is the signpost to the drive; in the second, the drive is the signpost to relationship.)

Finally, in psychoanalytic self psychology, the other person becomes important in determining the very structure and health of the self — in fact, there is no self without relationship. In this context, sexuality becomes a constituent of the self and is only used for its own sake when the self is intact. Only then can the other person be considered a true object, since otherwise, when the self is fragmenting, sexuality is utilized to provide interpersonal and intrapsychic glue, at which time the sexual partner is a selfobject, an intrapsychic constituent of the self, and not a separate person. The search for such glue may erotize relationships and lead to seduction. This leads me to the topic of the erotic transference and sexual acting out in therapy as a manifestation of the search for the *glutinum mundi* in the form of the selfobject experience.

The Erotic Transference

In the traditional psychoanalytic view, the erotic transference is a recreation of the Oedipal situation of childhood; the therapist is a new edition of the original parent. ("Erotic," here, means genital; the "erotized" transference refers to a pre-genital state of dependency, characterized by blatant erotic wishes and overt sexuality, a barely concealed regressive wish for the therapist to be a substitute parent with a loss of the "as if" quality of the more mature form.) Freud regarded such a transference as a resistance to the progress of therapy; the situation needed interpretation rather than gratification. It was feared that gratification would interfere with the recovery of repressed material, whereas frustration of the neurotic wish would allow it to be verbalized.

From the perspective of modern self psychology, it now seems that the historical worry about gratification and the need to frustrate the patient became overgeneralized to include all of the patient's developmental needs as they are directed at the therapist. But there is a big difference between satisfying a patient's wish for sex, which is unethical and a therapeutic disaster, and the meeting of legitimate selfobject needs for emotional responsiveness. These represent a new attempt at development, and to frustrate this category of the patient's demands merely retraumatizes him and prolongs the therapy. Such therapeutic behavior may be the cause of some interminable analyses, since it makes impossible the structural enhancement of the patient's self that would occur if his selfobject needs were responded to. But problems arise in therapy when selfobject needs are expressed in a manner that is sexually toned.

Rather than interpret all of the patient's erotized material as either Oedipal or due to early dependency needs which must be outgrown and relinquished, there is another, self psychological paradigm from which to view such a situation. This view suggests that not all sexual behavior is purely erotic in its intent. Early pre-Oedipal needs — for example, the need to be wanted and admired, can become confused with adult sexuality. Hugging, holding, and kissing — all very sensual behaviors — are ways in which the child is made to feel wanted, loved, and valued. Their intent is not primarily sexual. From this repertoire of responses to the child arise normal self esteem. Seen in this light, the patient's "Oedipal" wishes toward the therapist may actually hide the hope for acceptance and responsiveness — not for sexuality, which is only their vehicle. To respond to them with concrete sexuality is very damaging, as it would be to have sex with a child.

When the mirror need is sexualized, the patient's new and much desired experience of being seen, heard, and valued is so intense that his affection for the therapist feels erotic. In such a case, if the patient is either afraid of his sexual feelings or tries to seduce the therapist, the therapist only needs to tactfully explain that the situation is not primarily sexual. When the idealized parent imago is sexualized, the patient's feelings are actually akin to those of an excited child who wants to be a part of a powerful, loving parent. The child does not literally want sex with the parent, and the therapist must remember that the patient is looking for "glue," not sex. The sexualization of the transference is often a manifestation of the intensified need to fill a structural deficit within the self; it then represents a selfobject need which has become so intense it feels erotic. This is an example in the outer world of the well known fact that, in dreams, the psyche will often image an experience as sexual when it is intensely important. (We saw this process in the "Conjunction" picture of the *Rosarium*.)

To move for a moment to the intersubjectivist perspective, it is important to remember that, from within the patient's perspective or frame of reference, something in the therapist's tone of voice or facial expression may have seemed seductive, or may have actually been so unconsciously. In such a case, it is confusing and shaming to cast everything that happened in the therapeutic interaction in terms of a problem located entirely within the patient, as if the therapist contributed nothing. Sometimes the therapist is sexualizing the countertransference based on his or her own selfobject needs.

The overall point is that there are many reasons that a patient may try to seduce a therapist, or the therapist a patient, and these are not all Oedipal, nor are they all primarily due to a wish for sex. A few other reasons are suggested here, which are intended to illustrate the principle involved and do not exhaust the range of possibilites. The patient may try to seduce the therapist because she is terrified, and to be able to seduce him means that he is less dangerous because she is more in control of the situation. The patient may become seductive because the therapist has behaved in such a way as to disrupt the self-selfobject tie, thus threatening the integrity of the patient's self; to prevent herself from losing someone who has become important to her, she tries seduction as a way of restoring closeness (sexuality again seen as a fragmentation product). Or, erotism may be a manipulation, acting to try to trivialize the therapy and the therapist's work; here, it may be the result of envy or it may be a defense against the intensity of the patient's actual needs for the therapist. In all such cases, in order to understand the meaning of the patient's erotization of the relationship, it can be viewed as an encoded communication; to reveal its unconscious significance, the attempted seduction can be interpreted as if it were a dream, in which we have to discover what quality or inner figure it is so urgent for the dreamer to join with.

Even when we are sure that the patient's demands or seductive behavior are actually Oedipal in origin, the self psychological view modifies the traditional view of that situation. The healthy parental response to this developmental period, according to Kohut (1982), is not only like the myth of Oedipus, which is a pathological variant, but also like the myth of Odysseus and Telemachus. This story depicts intergenerational bonding and caring rather than competition. (In this mythologem, Odysseus is trying to avoid going to war by pretending to be insane; to test him, his infant son Telemachus is placed in the way of Odysseus' plough; he steers round the child, which is considered proof of his sanity. Kohut calls this the "semi-circle of mental health.") To view the Oedipal period as potentially normal rather than inevitably pathological makes a practical difference to our therapeutic attitude.

Kohut's attitude is very different from the classical view, which assumed that, when the child develops phase specific fantasies related to the maturation of sexual and aggressive drives, the same sex parent will only be viewed as a hostile rival. The actual behavior of the parents is then thought to be of less importance than the child's drive-dominated fantasies — typical of the child-blaming approach of this school of thought. But Kohut (1984) suggested that the Oedipal phase need not be pathological; if the child enters this period with an intact self, this stage offers the chance for a new set of experiences that may be normal. The child has intensified assertiveness and affection and expects that his selfobjects will respond to him with sustaining and affirming responses. A pathological complex results only when the parents respond poorly to the child's affection and assertiveness, for example, with competitiveness or excessive stimulation of the child. Or, if they cannot tolerate the child's sensuality, they may withdraw. These responses fragment the child, whose initially non-hostile assertiveness then disintegrates into raw aggression, or his sensual affection into raw sexuality. The young girl then fears confrontation by a sexually seductive, rather than affection-accepting, father. He may have difficulty being close to a coquettish child, or her mother may envy his attraction to his daughter. A boy fears confrontation by a sexually seductive mother, or a competitive-hostile father. The child's need is to be experienced as a whole self, enjoying his parent's pleasure at his growth. Only if this fails to occur does the child develop sexual or hostile fantasies which elaborate or contain his anxieties. If the parents respond appropriately and helpfully to the Oedipal phase child, with understanding and appropriate limits, there need be no excessive anxiety.

Similarly in therapy, when the patient's repressed or problematic sexuality begins to disinhibit, the therapist must not interfere. When the patient needs his or her sexuality to be affirmed, to have it treated as normal and valuable, it is damaging to interpret it as maliciously seductive, or bad and dangerous. Even if the patient is actually seductive, her unconscious hope, like that of the Oedipal child, is for the therapist not to be afraid, not to respond in kind with sexual overtures, but to understand what is happening. It is crucial that the therapist neither block the subjective experience of his or her own sexual feelings nor act them out. Inexperienced therapists who are afraid of acting out sometimes try to deny their own arousal. But if this blocking is perceived by the patient, it may convey the message that her sexuality is bad or shameful. Or, the patient may sense that the therapist is being hypocritical by pretending that nothing is happening between them; this is bad for the therapy. Such denial repeats the patient's childhood experience, in which her sexuality was attacked or used as a weapon against her. Instead, the sexual feelings must be acknowledged and contained, and, as necessary, the patient is told that there is a difference between talking about the meaning of sexual fantasies and feelings and acting them out. Desire is normal and grist for the therapeutic mill; action is harmful. The therapist can also block discussion of the patient's sexuality in specific areas in which the therapist has difficulty, such as incestuous feelings or homosexuality, by premature interpretation or dampening types of comments.

Patients who have difficulty with sexuality may handle this problem in many ways; one device is to see a Jungian rather than a Freudian because it is assumed that the emphasis of the therapy will then not disturb them. Jungians who do have this difficulty manage it by emphasizing the symbolic aspects of sexuality, such as the *coniunctio*, to protect themselves from its concrete physicality. It is certainly important to acknowledge that sexuality has its spiritual aspects, as is obvious from the frequent appearance of erotic imagery in mystical experience. The union of the soul with God is often depicted as sexual union. But there is a danger that, because of the risk of acting out, the therapeutic community may become too uncomfortable with the bodily aspects of sexuality, so that we again demonize the body or regard it as something to be fought with, as is the case in some religious traditions.

Schwartz-Salant (1984) points out that while ethical rules about proper behavior are useful, we must remember that they are essentially based on repression or suppression, and so, in the long run, are not as useful as consciousness. As is well known, to repress or to split off the shadow is eventually of limited usefulness because it then tends to leak out unconsciously or be projected. Only integration is of lasting value, which in this case means the integration of split off sexualized selfobject needs into the rest of the structures of the self. For the therapeutic community, this means that the real treatment of the problem of sexual acting out is for our trainees to have their own selfobject needs met within their own therapy. The blanket application of conventional morality and righteous indignation may be necessary to protect the helpless, but is not a psychological approach to the problem.

The Search for the Glutinum Mundi in Sexual Perversions and Enactments

Sometimes the search for the elusive substance needed to hold oneself together can manifest itself as an intense sexual need which seems addictive, such as a perversion. Disorders of the self appear in the form of this kind of sexual difficulty when early self-object failures become sexualized. This attitude leads to a very different dynamic formulation of psychosexual disorders than those of classical psychoanalysis. For example, the frustrated need to idealize may appear in distorted form as voyeurism, which is a sexualized fragment of the early need to admire the selfobject (Kohut 1971). The early need to be seen becomes a pathological need to exhibit oneself sexually.

When the self is seriously weakened, sexuality is stimulating enough to reorganize or revitalize the self. Sexual enactments such as compulsive masturbation allow an intense bodily experience to restore or maintain a fragile self-organization. Similarly, the Don Juan syndrome in men, or the compulsive need to seduce, which is seen in both therapists and patients, may be the result of a self-structure which is chronically depleted and constantly on the edge of collapsing. Incessant, self-reassuring sexual conquests temporarily counteract this danger and bolster self-esteem. Of course, they have no effect on the underlying problem, and so, like a drug that wears off, must be constantly repeated. Analogously, a woman whose response to the therapist is to immediately romaticize and sexualize the relationship may be trying to manage her low self-esteem and her constant dread of being rejected and uncared for. Or, the overt sexuality allows her to feel some temporary vitality, which deals with an inner deadness through the stimulation provided by being flirtatious; as a child, she tried to overcome her isolation and terrors by means of erotic fantasy, which she now tries to enact for the same reasons. Perhaps, her father was only interested in this aspect of herself, so that it seems to be her only source of responsiveness from others — there are many possible such patterns.

The Therapist's Vulnerabilities and Fears May Make Him Seductive

When the therapist is starved of his own selfobject needs, his personal life may be too burdensome for him to adequately meet the selfobject needs of his patients without the intrusion of his own difficulties. This situation predisposes him towards sexual acting out with patients. For example, if he desperately needs to be seen, but feels unappreciated, the advances of an admiring patient may be hard to resist. Or, if he needs to feel powerful, and the patient needs the care and protection of an idealized selfobject, this combination can feel very sexual. In other words, it is not sufficient to account for an erotic countertransference by saying that the patient has become an Oedipal object for the therapist. The therapist is engaged at deeper levels than this; his own pre-Oedipal archaic narcissistic needs may become sexualized. The need for recognition and enhancement of self-esteem, as well as the need to ward off depression and emptiness, may all lead to a seductive therapist. Here, the therapist is using the patient to meet his own needs, the so-called reverse selfobject situation, which occurs when narcissistic parents use their children to meet the parents' own needs. Of course, this exploits the patient and keeps her stuck in the same situation for which she came for help.

It is important to note that some therapists who act out with patients are actually re-enacting problems in their own therapy, in which they felt betrayed by their therapist. Just as the parent who was abused as a child may abuse his own children, so this kind of therapist may identify with the aggressor. This mechanism also applies when the therapist was actually abused in childhood; the patient becomes the abused child, and the therapist the abusing parent. He then uses the patient to try to master his own early trauma.

One further comment on the problem of child abuse as it is manifest in therapy. Where there has been incest in the patient's childhood, for several reasons there may be an unconscious attempt to re-experience this trauma within the transference. This may occur to try to communicate to the therapist what happened, or it may be a new attempt to master the trauma. Sometimes, at an unconscious infantile level, this is the only way in which the patient feels that she will get her selfobject needs met since this is what she had to go through to maintain the tie to her abusing parent. Whatever the reason, as P.J. Casement (1991, 327) points out, timing is important; if the therapist senses sexual abuse in the past, but interprets it too early, by forcing a sexual meaning onto non-sexual material, this may be experienced either as another assault or as seductive. But if the therapist ignores the issue for too long, or avoids it when it is present, he becomes the mother who refuses to acknowledge what is happening to the child. Finally, the appalling tendency of some therapists to invariably blame the whole issue on the patient's endogenous fantasy needs little comment, except to point out its defensive function within the therapist.

The Case of Anne

Anne is a highly intelligent, well-educated woman of forty who came to therapy trying to decide whether to end an affair with an older married man. Since the age of sixteen, she has consistently seduced and had affairs with such men. All the men she has been involved with are damaged in some important way; she feels that men who are intact could not possibly be interested in her, and she never finds them interesting. All of her conquests are men who need Anne's help for their own development and who are very grateful for this help. Her message to them is: "Let me be crucial to you, and I will make you happy." Anne sees herself as the savior of needy men. Their woundedness is essential for Anne to feel any erotic attraction, and only when she is suffering and self-sacrificing in a relationship is her sexuality stimulated. The sex itself is not as important as the man's fascination with, and need for, her; she needs his rapture. "I submit to him, but I control him at the same time. Sex is only the vehicle to make him fascinated with me. Sex disguises what I want so it looks like something they want." Her job is to redeem the man; this is why she is here, but at the same time paradoxically "it's never really for me."

When her current lover, Charlie, is with her, he experiences his youth and vitality enlivened by her; it is like a new springtime for him. In his presence, Anne feels special — the one who fans his creative flame; she is truly seen for who she is — interesting and exciting. When they are apart, she is depressed and empty (the addictive quality is evident here). Anne was initially attracted to Charlie when she noticed a physical disability; when she discovered his impotence, he became irresistible — the more so as she was actually able to help him with this longstanding problem. In bed, both enjoy whispering long, exciting sexual fantasies to each other, in which the main point is for normal boundaries to be violated. He has incest fantasies about his mother, she about her father. His are also about sex between grandfathers and grandaughters, or about sex with young native girls on a beach — they always involve the woman's loss of virginity. The fact that Charlie would violate a boundary for her makes him additionally exciting.

Anne's father was chronically and severely depressed. During her childhood, he spent most of his time in bed, rarely paid her any attention, and generally behaved as if she did not exist. She would feel as if she became invisible in his presence. The rare moments in which he acknowledged her stand out in her memory like brilliant flashes of light, but they were all too few and too brief. However, all along she recognized his misery and knew that she could have made him happy, "unlike my horrible mother. But he rarely let me do it; when I meet men who let me do it all the time it is intoxicating." Charlie is like her father in that he is also chronically depressed, but with a core vitality that she, only she and not his wife, can bring to life — and he loves it when she does so. Then, "it is as if I am able to bring my father back to life in Charlie."

This situation repeats both Oedipal and pre-Oedipal difficulties. Here, I am concerned to try to show how Anne's early self-object needs to be seen and valued became so sexualized. Anne remembers her childhood attraction to her father who was overtly exhibitionistic in that he would briefly, but repeatedly, appear nude in the house. At the same time, she suffered from his indifference to her, and she would try to fix his misery, while competing with mother for his attention. Her sexual attraction to him was colored by his obvious woundedness. Her Oedipal fantasies, his need to be helped, her need to compete with mother in the attempt to help, and her intense need to be seen by him all seem to have fused in the making of her father complex. The important point is that she is not just interested in seducing older, father-like men; her sexuality is only awakened by her need to revitalize and be revitalized. This is what she seeks, rather than sex for its own sake. When she is seen, she is alive; otherwise she is inert and empty. The sexual component in her seductions is secondary and is only used in the search for selfobject glue — it is minimally important in its own right.

Conclusion: Back to the Coniunctio and the Glutinum Mundi as the Link Between Body and Soul

To bring us back to alchemy, "The Naked Truth" (Figure 10) from the *Rosarium* series (Jung 1966, 16: 237) exemplifies why Jung correctly intuited the importance of these woodcuts, although I suggest that he should not have altered their original sequence. In Christian iconography, the holy spirit often appears in the form of the dove, for example, at the baptism of Jesus. The meaning of this bird has always been to stress innocence and purity of motive rather than power — an important therapeutic consideration. In ancient Greece, the dove was sacred to both Aphrodite and Demeter, an interesting and important archetypal combination, also relevant to the problem of the erotized need for a maternal selfobject. The dove heralded heavenly news; as they performed their divinations, Zeus' oracular priestesses listened to the cooing of doves. The caption says: *"Spiritus est qui unificat,"* or "spirit is what unites [or unifies]." The dove indicates the descent of spirit from above; spirit means an archetypal ordering principle, so that I understand this image to mean that a new organization is to occur. This will be guided not only by personal wishes, which are the overt reason that a person comes to therapy, but also by transpersonal factors. As M. Jacoby (1984) points out, the love that will emerge is not only earthly, but a form of *agape*, intended to bring compassionate help to the other person. It is directed towards the birth of a divine child as a result of the interaction of the human and the divine.

In summary, Jung was correct that the desire for the *coniunctio*, or union with another, underlies the transference, but it is only recently that it has been possible to delineate the details of the selfobject mechanisms by which this is brought about at the personal level. I have argued that these mechanisms are part of an innate, Self-induced urge to completion. The need for a selfobject is a manifestation of the transcendent function as it appears within relationships, leading us to search for a relationship that will supply the necessary interpersonal and intrapsychic glue. The

Figure 10: The Naked Truth

Source: Jung (1966, 16: 237)

problem for the therapist is that the *coniunctio* yields what Jung calls "kinship libido," or the sense that we belong to the same family. Thus, we must remember that archetypally the therapeutic pair is an endogamous couple even though they may feel that they are unrelated at first. Obviously, therefore, the relationship has the potential to be permeated with incestuous feelings. Herein lies an important paradox, which is that the union must be felt psychologically, but not enacted physically. Therefore, it seems that there are two competing claims; on the one hand, we have the *coniunctio*, an essential archetypal experience that spans the spectrum from the somatic to the spiritual, and, on the other, we have an equally important archetypal prohibition — the incest taboo — against its physical enactment. We do not object to the intrapsychic manifestations of the *coniunctio*, such as the selfobject experience, dreams of union, deeply shared feelings and imagery, moments of profound understanding, and so on. Yet the *coniunctio* is also sometimes felt in the body as a prohibited urge to concrete sexuality. Why, then, is the body so involved? What is the resolution of this paradox within psychotherapy?

One solution seems to be that the alchemists described the *glutinum mundi* as the connection between body and soul. I take this to mean that when we meet the patient's selfobject needs, we allow aspects of the Self that have so far never been properly recognized or valued to embody within him. To the extent that who we are archetypally is recognized in this way by another person, the Self can embody as what we refer to as soul. That is, previously unknown elements of the Self become internalized as felt experiences, or attributes, that the individual can own as "really me" — they then belong to the personal self. Such recognition and attunement thereby provide a mechanism by which the soul becomes linked with the body in development.

For example, a most important selfobject function is to help the child integrate affect into the organization of his self structures. It is well known that affect is the effect of the archetype in the body; the child's experience of such intense affect requires an attuned adult response so that the child can be helped to cope with it and not be overwhelmed. This means that the selfobject must assist in the affirmation and acceptance of the child's affect, as well as help him differentiate it, so that defenses against it are

not necessary. If the selfobject provides such help with containment and working through of affect, it becomes well structural-
ized and does not threaten to disintegrate the self. The sexualization of the selfobject need also ensures that it is embodied; by
sexualizing the selfobject situation, the psyche makes sure that
we realize that something important is happening. Hence the
involvement of the body is essential for recognition purposes. Our
therapeutic task is therefore to understand the overall intention of
the psyche when the selfobject experience is sexualized, remembering that events in the body can also be regarded as part of a
complex. This has to be respected and understood at a symbolic as
well as a literal level, and like any complex, it cannot be unconsciously allowed to take over the therapy.

To summarize the importance of the notion of the *glutinum
mundi*, I can do no better than to reiterate Kohut's (1977, 287)
quote from Eugene O'Neill's play, *The Great God Brown*: "Man is
born broken. He lives by mending. The grace of God is glue."

Note

[1] Fordham uses the term "self object" (written as two separate words) to
mean a part object, or a need satisfying object, such as the breast, at a
stage before the baby can symbolize. He contrasts the self object with
early, bad, or not-self objects. In this system, the self object is eventually
destroyed in order to create a symbol. Or, the self object is used, in
distinction from real objects, to perceive reality before the infant has
adequate reality testing of his own.

Bibliography

Casement, P.J. 1991. *Learning From the Patient*. New York: Guilford
Press.

Fordham, M. 1976. *The Self and Autism*. London: Heinemann.

——. 1985. *Explorations Into the Self*. London: Academic Press.

Jung, C.G. 1966. *The Practice of Psychotherapy*. Collected Works 16.
New York: Bollingen Foundation and Pantheon Books

——. 1968. *Psychology and Alchemy*. Collected Works 12. Princeton,
New Jersey : Princeton University Press

——. 1970. *Mysterium Coniunctionis*. Collected Works 14. New York:

Bollingen Foundation and Pantheon Books.

———. 1973. *Letters 1.* Edited by G. Adler and A. Jaffé and translated by R.F.C. Hull. Princeton. New Jersey: Princeton University Press.

Kohut, H. 1971. *The Analysis of the Self.* New York: International Universities Press.

———. 1977. *The Restoration of the Self.* New York: International Universities Press.

———. 1982. "Introspection, Empathy, and the Semi-Circle of Mental Health." *International Journal of Psychoanalysis* 63: 395-407.

———. 1984. *How Does Analysis Cure?*, edited by Arnold Goldberg and Paul Stepansky. Chicago: University of Chicago Press.

Jacoby, M. 1984. *The Analytic Encounter.* Toronto: Inner City Books.

McLean, Adam. 1980. *The Rosary of the Philosophers.* Grand Rapids, Michigan: Magnum Opus Sourceworks.

Samuels, A. 1989. *The Plural Psyche.* London: Routledge.

Schwartz-Salant, N. 1984. "Archetypal Factors Underlying Sexual Acting-Out in the Transference / Countertransference Process." In *Transference / Countertransference.* Wilmette, Illinois: Chiron Publishers.

———. 1989. *The Borderline Personality: Vision and Healing.* Wilmette, Illinois: Chiron Publishers.

Stolorow, R.D., B. Brandschaft and G.E. Atwood. 1987. *Psychoanalytic Treatment: An Intersubjective Approach.* Hillside, New Jersey: Analytic Press.

Stolorow, R.D. and G.E. Atwood. 1992. *Contexts of Being.* New York: Academic Press.

Wolf, E. 1988. *Treating the Self.* New York: Guilford.

Chapter 7

Mining/Fishing/Analysis: Seduction as Alchemical Extractio

Ronald Schenk

When I was asked to write a paper on the theme of seduction and alchemy, I had just entered into a classical Freudian analysis on the couch. I had made this commitment for several reasons, one of which was to explore the role of seduction in my life — how I seduce and am seduced. As a Jungian analyst, and perhaps because of the turbulent history of the subject in Jungian circles, I felt a need to extract myself from the Jungian approach in order to get "on top" of the issue. I soon realized, however, that I had been seduced by something else — the couch itself which, with its horizontal position, carried me into completely unexpected places. It seems that we can never get away from the business of seduction in analysis.

As we talk about seduction, we are seducing and being seduced all the time. How does this happen? What is the shadow of morality that exists behind seduction? Why is it that the word is so consistently the object of a pejorative attitude and using the word in this way carries with it an unassailable sense of moral rectitude and authority? Is this moralizing attitude associated with the sexual overtones of the word, and where do they come from? Why is seduction of particular concern in the history of depth psychology?

Historically, seduction is a cornerstone of depth psychology. Much controversy has existed regarding the seductive effects of techniques which were the precursors or psychotherapy — animal magnetism during the late eighteenth century and hypnosis throughout the nineteenth century. Such controversy resulted in the formation of ethics committees and commissions, which anticipated current controversies surrounding psychotherapy and seduction. In 1882, Joseph Breuer prematurely terminated his treatment of "Anna O.," the first case of psychotherapy as "talking cure," fearful of the seductive influence of the work on both himself and his patient. Freud based one of his fundamental techniques on seduction, the analysis of the transference, using the patient's erotic feelings toward the analyst as a means of therapeutic change (Freud 1915). Jung feared "seduction" by the voice of a female figure from his unconscious who considered his work as art (Jung 1965, 185-87). In his major work on transference, he established the process involved in the psychologically erotic coupling between analyst and client as the basis of therapeutic change (Jung [1946] 1954). In recent years, the seductive actions of Freud and Jung in relation to their patients and even extended families have been discussed in terms of both the moral issues involved and the bearing they have on the founding principles and techniques of depth psychology (Kerr 1993; Goodheart 1984; Carentaldo 1982).[1]

The clinical setting provides an arena for many forms of seduction. First are the sexual seductions toward which we aim our ethical formulations (Schwartz-Salant 1984; Rutter 1991; Springer 1995). Next are the non-sexual, but equally destructive, crossings of therapeutic boundaries that can occur with the analyst's interaction with clients outside of the therapeutic setting. Finally, there are the subtle seductions that occur in the everyday interaction of analyst and patient. Patients seduce analysts with sickness. Patients seduce analysts with their intelligence, emotions, and charisma. Analysts seduce patients with techniques: requests for dreams and active imaginations, dream interpretations, amplifications, sand trays, pictures, labels and concepts. Patients seduce analysts with compliance. Analysts seduce patients with understanding; patients seduce analysts with the "search for meaning." Patients seduce analysts with idealizations and compliance. Analysts seduce patients with interventions or with silence. Analysts seduce patients with answers; patients seduce analysts with questions. Patients seduce analysts with confessions and "juicy" material. Analysts seduce patients with self-disclosures. Analysts seduce patients by making trauma literal or metaphorical. Patients seduce analysts with stoicism and victimization.[2] Patients seduce analysts into terminations, either premature or prolonged. Analysts seduce patients into terminations, either premature or prolonged.

Any kind of behavior in the clinical setting can take on the quality of seduction. The experience of seduction is of an attraction that catches our fancy, desire, or appetite, and leads us away to a place of revealed discomfort, suffering, or loss, where we feel tricked and betrayed. In response to our fears of seduction, we strive to distance ourselves — on the high road or the straight road or the long road, all of which carry our comfortable feeling of right-mindedness, innocence, and moral rectitude.

If Jungians tend to be particularly prone to seduction, it is also Jungians who might see through to a deeper sense of seduction. Do not the myths and legends and fairy tales teach us that being enticed away from the path, away from the control of a dominant position, is exactly what is needed for the evolving soul of the protagonist? The mother-daughter configuration is deepened through Persephone's attraction to the narcissus flower, and Little Red Cap is strengthened through being tricked by the wolf. Anchises is horrified to find that he has slept with a goddess, but Aphrodite reveals to him the mysteries of his life. The knight is led off the path by the bounding deer, but that is when adventures start to happen. Shiva is drawn out of his meditation by Shakti, and the universe unfolds.

Here is a personal story (and as Jungians know, there is nothing more seductive than the personal). I once received a phone call from an old friend from the southwest — a dancing, drinking, old desert rat — a throwback to the beatniks of the fifties — a former radical environmentalist and a landscape painter in the abstract expressionist school of his teachers, Turner, de Kooning, and Hoffmann. My dionysian friend, a fellow aging puer, is perpetually wandering, "looking for that long-lost shaker of salt," incessantly trying to find a place to settle down, always imagining the ideal homestead around the corner or on the horizon — and selling me on it. This time, he was raving about property in southern Arizona, where he already had several artist friends, where Gary Snyder and Lawrence Ferlinghetti were supposedly buying homes, and where there was a gallery with a sympathetic owner in which he could finally have a base from which to sell his paintings. The property, he proclaimed, was near the desert mountains, with a beautiful view and a stream running down off the mountains — in short, "ocean front property in Arizona."

Now, some desire in me always manages to get caught by my friend and his boyish enthusiasm and idealism, his puerile pursuits, his fifties black and white simplicity contrasting with the deep colors and mythical themes of his paintings, his yearning for family and community that seem perpetually elusive, his anger at the establishment — concealing his underlying insecurity; his dedication to his work; his struggles for money; and his passion for the desert, mountains, and sea of the west. He assured me that he was getting a great deal financially, but needed somebody to go in with him. I was the first of his friends to whom he was making this offer; how could I possibly refuse?

Caught by the smell of a Kerouac/Cassidy adventure, I said, "Sure, why the hell not?" The next thing I knew, I was going down the road, my wife and I bickering like Lucille Ball and Bob Hope from a 1950s comedy, setting out to discover my new acquisition. When we got to our destination, I found myself the proud owner of ten acres of tumbleweed in a desert flatland. The "mountain stream" turned out to be a dried up wash that ran, at best, once every three years. My friend had sabotaged any chance of establishing himself in the community or selling his paintings by indulging in a drunken orgy at his opening show, offending friends and potential patrons alike, and then taking flight. I was hanging high and dry with my pants down — seduced.

Something in me had also been exposed, though — led away, extracted, drawn out to drink — something that desired the moisture of feeling for a friend and for creative expression, something that wanted home and community away from the dry, rigid, isolated, saturnine desert into which I had let my psyche settle in everyday urban life.

There are many stories from fields outside of depth psychology to show how seduction works in a therapeutic way. Carl Whitaker, a family therapist who based his work on the principle of creativity, always practiced with a co-therapist. One of his images for family therapy came from a group of South Sea Island natives that fishes for octopus in pairs. A fisherman offers himself as bait and dives down to the bottom of the reef with a rope in tow, becomes entangled with the octopus, and is pulled up by his partner who captures the octopus. Likewise, in family therapy, one therapist gets entangled in the family pathology and becomes "crazy" so that the identified patient can be relieved of this burden. The craziness, now overt and carried by an outsider, can be revealed as a logical part of the family's dynamics and thera- pized by the co-therapist. Likewise, tribes in Africa have been known to hunt for alligators by having a man swim into the river as bait with a rope around him. When the alligator comes in hot pursuit, the man is hauled in by the rope. His comrades ream the alligator with a sharpened log through its open mouth, turn it on its back, and kill it by mauling its soft underbelly. These are both images of what happens in psychotherapy when a complex is teased out into the open through the dynamics of the transference and countertransference. The problem for us as therapists, to para- phrase Jung, is that at times we do not know whether we are the fishermen reeling in the line, or the octopus getting sliced up, or the alligator being beaten on the belly.

The dry workings of institutional life would seem to be a strange home for the power of seduction, but here it can easily be seen in the seductive qualities of power in decision making. Seduction by the power of decision-making can be thought of in terms of alchemy which presents the dynamics of life in terms of working with "matter," specifically metals. Decision-making is a function which the alchemists would locate in the sphere of Jupiter, which, in turn, has tin as its earthly representative. James Hillman has used an alchemical story about the mining of tin that enables us to see more deeply into seduction as a natural process.

In a place in the far West where tin is found, there is a spring from which it rises from the earth like water. When the inhab- itants of the region see that the tin is about to spread beyond its source, they select a young girl, remarkable for her beauty, and place her entirely nude below the source, in a hollow of the ground, in order that it, the tin, shall be enamored.... It springs out of the ground at the young girl, seeking to seize her, but she escapes by running rapidly while the young people keep near her, holding axes in their hands. As soon as they see it approach the young girl, they strike and cut the flow of metal and it comes of itself into the hollow and of itself solidifies and hardens. They cut it into bars and use it. And this is why they call the water of the river, the mercury drawn from the tin.[3]

Here, we have a sense of the action of seduction serving as a separation of a particular metal from the "mass" of the earth and a sense that its subsequent entrapment or suffering, its hardening and being cut into bars, is what allows for it to be accessed. What we call seduction, the alchemists called chemistry, and Hillman calls strip mining.

In these stories, I am trying to show how the notion of seduction can be seen as furthering psychological processes. Seduction seems to reveal distinct essences in the service of an overall purpose. In its origins, seduction meant to lead away from a central or dominating position or system. The word, "seduction," can be divided into its two Latin components, "se" and "duc," meaning respectively "away" and "to lead." "Seduce" means to lead away, to draw aside, to lead out of harm's way, as well as to lead astray, to move away or withdraw, to separate off from family or society, to withdraw mentally, to draw apart, to divide or split, to divert from allegiance.

While the association of seduction with sexual intercourse actually did not come about until the sixteenth century in Puritan England, there is an Aphrodisian element in the etymology of the root "duc," which implies connecting, such as in duct, viaduct, and conductor. (Copper, the metal of Venus, is also the metal of conduction.) "Duc" gives rise also to words like "educe," "induce," "deduce," "reduce," all leading somewhere in erotic connection — whether out, in, down, away, or back to the same place.

"Seduction," in its original meanings, seems to be Jungian in more ways than the one we usually hear about. The fundamental sense of the word alludes to the same themes as the Jungian notion of individuation, that is, as a way of moving away from the beaten path or the herd, or eschewing obedience to a collective or ego-centered standpoint, and following a unique, peculiar, or solitary way. The association of the root "duc" with our word, "educate," meaning "to lead out," implies, as Jungian psychology does, that there is something to be learned from the suffering of separation.

Alchemy invites us to think further of seduction as a "leading away," which is in keeping with Jungian thought. One of the identities of alchemists was that they were "workers in metals."

Paracelsus defined alchemy simply as the "set purpose, intention and subtle endeavor to transmute the kinds of metals from one to another" (Waite 1976, 16). For the alchemists, metals were seeds that had a life of their own, generated under the influence of the planets and other heavenly bodies. Each metal had a corresponding heavenly body, the qualities of which it reflected: quicksilver was an emanation of Mercury; copper, of Venus; iron, Mars; tin, Jupiter; lead, Saturn; silver, the moon; and finally, gold was the manifestation of the sun. The planets were considered to be spirits embodied; the metals were bodies enspirited.

The metals as animate bodies went through various processes naturally — they lived, thrived, desired, had lovers and enemies; were tortured, killed, resuscitated, and transmuted — all of which corresponded to the various operations in alchemy. Hermes Trismegitus said, "He who perfects these operations creates a new world" (Waite 1976, 85). In other words, each metal was a cosmological domain or a psychological "world," with a life and personality of its own. The work of alchemy was to help in the transmutation of these worlds.

Each metal had a particular quality of relationship to the other metals (Bacon 1975, 3). Silver "wants nothing, save a little fixation, color, and weight," while gold "wants nothing." Lead, the metal of Saturn, "is an unclean and imperfect body, engendered of Argent-vive impure (another name for Mercury) not fixed, earthy, drossy, somewhat white outwardly, and red inwardly.... It wants purity, fixation, color and firing."

Copper, the metal of Venus, is also an "unclean and imperfect body, engendered of Argent-vive, impure, not fixed, earthy, burning, red not clear, and of the like Sulphur. It wants purity, fixation, and weight." Here, the psychological truth of the attraction of depression and passion for each other, which is expressed in Greek mythology in the marriage of Hepahaistos and Aphrodite, is depicted in the desire of lead for color and firing and in the desire of copper for weight.

The alchemical idea that metals, as living beings, relate with other metals gives us a psychological language for the dynamics of human relationship. Hillman, again, points us to an alchemical story which helps us to understand how our human interactions can most psychologically be depicted through alchemical imagery

(Hillman 1982, 133-35).

In his novel, *The Rainbow*, D.H. Lawrence describes the encounter of a young woman, Ursula, who harbors a deep discontentment with the pent-up life she leads in rural England, with a visiting young soldier, Skrebensky, with whom she develops a romantic relationship. Skrebensky leaves but returns a few months later for wedding festivities associated with the late summer harvest.

This time, things are different. Skrebensky creates a "deadness" around her, in contrast to the invigoration of the festive surroundings, and she wants to let go, not only from him, but to be gone from the earth. Lawrence writes:

> As the dance surged heavily on, Ursula was aware of some influence looking in upon her.... Some powerful glowing sight was looking right into her.... She turned and saw a great white moon ... her breast opened to it.... She stood filled with the full moon, offering herself.... She wanted the moon to fill in to her, she wanted more, more communion with the moon, consummation (1976, 317).

Here, Lawrence locates Ursula's desire and her sense of imprisonment alchemically in the orbit of the moon. She has not been allowed access to moon worship or lunacy; she has not been getting enough moonshine.

Lawrence gives us clues that Skrebensky, the soldier, manifests the world of iron, of Mars. He puts his arm around Ursula, leads her away, and covers her with his cloak. He feels like a "lodestone" to her, taking on a quality of "the dross," "dark, impure magnetism." A "strange rage" fills her, and her hands feel like "blades of destruction." She walks toward the moon, "silver-white herself."

Lawrence becomes more specific; it is the salt in Ursula that has been imprisoned. As Jung goes to great lengths to tell us in the *Mysterium Coniunctionis*, salt, the principle of fixation, is intricately related with the moon, with lunar psychology (Jung [1955-56] 1959d, 14: 183-85). The couple begins to dance again, and Ursula feels a "fierce, white, cold passion in her heart." The struggle between them intensifies. Skrebensky presses his body on her and wishes to set a bond around her and compel her to his will, but she is "cold and unmoved as a pillar of salt." Ursula's salt is becoming empowered, empowered through its connection with the moon.

> She seemed a beam of gleaming power. She was afraid of what she was. Looking at him, at his shadowy, unreal wavering presence a sudden lust seized her, to lay hold of him and tear him and make him into nothing.... And timorously, his hands went over her, over the salt, compact brilliance of her body.... If he could but net her brilliant, cold, salt-burning body in the soft iron of his own hands, net her, capture her, hold her down, how madly he would enjoy her.... And always she was burning and brilliant and hard as salt, and deadly.... Even, in his frenzy he sought for her mouth with his mouth, though it was like putting his face into some awful death ... hard and fierce she had fastened upon him, cold as the moon and burning as a fierce salt. Till gradually his warm, soft iron yielded, yielded and she was there fierce, corrosive seething with his destruction, seething like some cruel corrosive salt around the last substance of his being, destroying him, destroying him in the kiss. And her soul crystallized with triumph, and his soul was dissolved with agony and annihilation. So she held him there, the victim, consumed, annihilated. She had triumphed: he was not any more (Lawrence 1976, 319-20).[4]

Through the imagery of alchemy, Lawrence is giving us a more precise psychological language, the seduction of iron by salt, to replace the language of popular psychology ("gender conflict") and Jungian psychology ("masculine" and "feminine"). What we call the "victim," is imagined here as iron, and what we call the "perpetrator," is salt. We can well imagine from what Bacon tells us of iron — that it wants fusion and purity — how it would be "led away" from its base or its mass to fuse with salt. Here is an image of the psyche depicted as a matrix of substances which attract and repel, love and war, triumph and lose, live and die.

In alchemical language, the operations which are featured in what we call seduction are *separatio*, and, more particularly, *extractio*. *Extractio*, meaning drawn, pulled, or dragged outside of, is the operation performed by the alchemists, wherein each metal is separated from the imperfection of the others. Paracelsus informs us: "By extraction, the pure is separated from the impure, the spirit and the quintessence from their body" (Waite 1976, 163).

Extraction brings forth essence.

The suffering or sense of being tricked that is innate to the experience of seduction comes from the fact that extraction often is a form of *mortificatio* or death. Paracelsus, again, tells us that the "transposition of the metals (occurs) from one death to another" (Waite 1976, 9). Cinnabar, for example, was mortified mercury, while brass was mortified copper. This is like saying that individuation is a series of particular deaths. Whatever condition the psyche is in is the death of another condition.

Seduction through extraction and mortification is illustrated in the film, *The Crying Game*, a film depicting a complex matrix of seductions and counter-seductions. Jody, a black soldier in the British army in Ireland, is seduced by Jude, a female member of the IRA, and is captured. Jody, in turn, seduces one of his Irish captors, Fergus, into various gratifications, but is fatally seduced himself into an abortive attempt at escape. Fergus, meanwhile, has been seduced by Jody into taking up relationship with Jody's girlfriend, Dil, a relationship he maintains even after Dil is ironically revealed to be, in Fergus' words, "something else" from what he had expected.

The core of the film is a parable about a frog who is seduced by a scorpion into taking the scorpion across a river, only to have the scorpion sting him halfway across. As they both sink, the frog cries out, "Why did you sting me, Scorpion, now we will both drown?" The scorpion replies, "I can't help it, it's in my nature." In alchemical language, the film tells us that there are different aspects to our nature that are drawn out of us through seduction, and what is specifically revealed in Fergus' nature is not only his ability to be caring in an atmosphere of hostility, but his ability to sacrifice himself in the service of eros for a man, a statement to the contemporary collective that speaks of the love of men for men outside of sexual involvement.

With the alchemical basis of seduction established, we can now gain a further sense of how seduction serves analysis as a fundamental mode, by looking at the history of the operation of extraction in depth psychology. In his book, *The Discovery of the Unconscious*, Henri Ellenberger traces the emergence of dynamic psychiatry to the year 1775 and to the clash between Johan Joseph Gassner (1727-1779) and Franz Anton Mesmer (1734-1815). Father

Gassner, a country priest, was famous in Europe for his healing powers through the practice of exorcism. Gassner would evoke the symptoms of a disease in his patient and then extract them out of the patient's body with ritualized declarations.

While Gassner performed his cures in the name of Christian faith, Mesmer, through the vision of rationalism and science, saw in them the workings of a physical element. He initiated a new method of healing, called animal magnetism and based on the idea that a physical, magnetic fluid flowed within individuals and throughout the universe. Disease occurred in individuals through an imbalance in this fluid. (Jungians will see the similarity to Jung's theory of libido as psychic energy and his notion of the compensatory nature of the psyche.) Mesmer would correct the imbalance by attaching magnets to the patient's body. When the patient swallowed a preparation containing iron, he or she would exhibit morbid symptoms that would subsequently disappear, as if being led away or seduced by the magnets. Mesmer concluded that the experience of magnetic streams could not have been elicited by magnets alone, but by an "essentially different agent," produced by fluid accumulated in his own person. Eventually, Mesmer sat with his patients, pressed the patient's thumbs in his hands, looked fixedly into the patient's eyes, and then touched various symptomatic parts of the patient's body, allowing for the symptoms to disappear. (Here is the precursor, not only for psychoanalytic catharsis and transference, but for knee-to-knee Jungian analysis.)

In the history of depth psychology, the chain of healing procedures transformed from generation to generation, while retaining a common element of extraction. Animal magnetism was the forerunner of hypnosis, wherein the hypnotizer would elicit morbid symptoms which were then extracted through suggestion. Hypnosis, in turn, preceded psychoanalysis, in which a transferential neurosis was elicited in the patient and "projected" out onto the analyst. Jungian analysis, in turn, made this "projection" meaningful, both causally and spiritually, through the technique of amplification. I am suggesting that in the history of psychological healing from alchemy, through exorcism to animal magnetism, hypnosis, psychoanalysis, and, finally, Jungian analysis, there runs a common thread of interaction between doctor and patient.

In the language of alchemy, this interaction is characterized by an aspect of the patient's psychological "nature" being "extracted" through a form of seduction on the part of the alchemist, exorcist, magnetizer, hypnotist, or analyst. We now refer to this interaction in relation to psychotherapy in terms of transference / countertransference, the bi-polar field (note the allusion to magnetism), or the wounded healer archetype, all of which are seen as constellated between doctor and patient.

Jung describes the connection between psychotherapy and *extractio:*

> We shall, by carefully analyzing every fascination, extract from it a portion of our personality, like a quintessence, and slowly come to recognize that we meet ourselves time and again in a thousand disguises on the path of life ([1946] 1954, 16: 318).

We have now come around to the opposite attitude from which we started. The "path" is, now, not something to avoid being seduced away from; rather it consists of reflections upon the various seductions, fascinations, or fallings away that occur in our experience.

Jung describes the attracting nature of the psyche in terms of "fascination," a term which was at one time a word used to describe what we now call "psychotherapy" (Ellenberger 1970, 151). The fascinosum is a favorite concept of Jung's, which he borrowed from Rudolph Otto, who used it to describe the entrancing quality of the "holy" (1923, 31-40). Jung uses the term to describe the attracting quality of unconscious contents on the conscious mind. The root of the word "fascination" refers to smell, so that the erotic attraction involved in the process of extraction is not necessarily one of the genitals but of the nose. Jung describes consciousness as being like dogs "scenting" the unconscious ([1950] 1959b, 9: 378). Paraphrasing David Miller, we might say that seduction leads us away to an intuitive, bodily, vigorous, earthy, pungently aromatic form of knowing through "nosing," where "the nose knows" or the nose "has to be faced" (1981, 61-88).

In other words, in clinical practice the therapist will often proceed most therapeutically, not when imposing a conceptual model onto the situation, but when closely following or "sniffing" actual experience. An example of the former would be the use of the notion of "projection," an unfortunate metaphor which gives a sense of certainty to the user which is not validated in actual clinical experience. "Projection" presupposes a Cartesian mind with a subjective source from which objects are "thrown forth" onto an inanimate world. If I say something is projected, I am positing one living entity — an enclosed soul — but if I say something is extracted through seduction, I am assuming a dual source of energy, that which attracts and also the attracted. Each has a pull on the other.

Jung stated that projections have a "hook." To complete the image, we would say that hooks hold living bait as attraction and are attached to lines which have living entities who reel them in. With extraction, the emphasis would not be on the "throwing forth" or "taking back" of projections, but on the reciprocal flow of attracting and attracted, where the establishment of a logocentric base or source is not only impossible, but irrelevant. In 1934 Jung made this startling statement in regard to the attracting nature of the anima (and also anticipating object relations theory):

> The word "projection" is not really appropriate, for nothing has been cut out of the psyche, rather, the psyche has attained its present complexity by a series of acts of introjection (1959a, 9: 25).

The idea of a reciprocal flow of energy would have uncomfortable implications for analysts and therapists. Embracing this dynamic, we would be forced to abandon the role of omniscient observer or the repository of projections that are brought to light and "taken back" by the patient. We would also have to abandon the sense of ourselves as "surgeons," the image used by both Freud and Jung to represent delving into the depths of the psychic body. Instead, we would be forced to assume the role of the "hooker," the seducer that attracts concealed elements of psychic life from the patient.

Recently, I had a patient whose fears regarding relationship carried over into the analysis. He was a salesman who historically had been seduced and molested in several ways by his mother. His work and social life were governed by a seductive mode in which he seemed to give others what they wanted, while maintaining an underlying control of the relationship. He reported feeling uncomfortable with my silence, said he could not read me, and did not feel I was helping him to set up goals and take specific steps to solve his problems. He felt that I was withholding knowledge from him and suspected that I had a hidden agenda. Quoting from a recent popular Jungian-oriented book on male psychology, he accused me of being a "black magician" who withheld knowledge for the sake of power. He angrily questioned how I could be a Jungian analyst and not be overtly helping him to solve his problems with archetypal amplifications of the sort offered in this book.

In fact, my patient was right; my silence was seducing him by teasing out his anxiety which, in turn, concealed painful, repressed material in various forms. I later lost him to the analysis when I became seduced into a more active and supportive role during a time of great stress. This role duplicated the role his mother played, which, although gratifying in the immediate sense, brought with it underlying anxiety regarding control and engulfment. Because I had stopped being the hooker and become the mother, it was impossible for him to address this anxiety with me.

In talking about seduction and psychotherapy, I have been using metaphors such as the mining of magnets and the fascination of fishing. I have also used the language of desire with words like "attract" and "arouse," "tempt" and "tease." In doing so, I am trying to bring about a different sense of eros than that which is governed by the preconceptions of puritanism and which provides the ground of our conventional, pejorative understanding of seduction.

I am also attempting to show that psychological understanding emerges, not so much through the classical dynamics of proportion or the mechanical dynamics of rationalism, both of which we are relying upon when we use conceptual systems such as typology, the union of opposites, and the compensatory nature of the psyche to explain individuation. Rather, I am suggesting that the understanding which occurs in psychotherapy emerges in the emanations that occur through the dynamics of eros. Different aspects of the soul appear in the world through the movement of different kinds of loves.

We find a basis of tradition for the idea of eros as the mover of soul in Neoplatonism and Hinduism. For Plato (1961a), it is the love of beauty that stimulates the growth of the soul's wings and with which the soul flies passionately into the world. Plato (1961b) saw all understanding as coming about through the soul's attraction for earthly beauty which starts with the beauty of the body. In the neoplatonic tradition, eros is that which binds the different aspects of the universe, imagined as a fountain, animated by a circular flow of love from the source to the various levels of emanation and back again. The source loves its creations, and the created long for their origins. Eros, then, is the purposive, the striving, the intending of universal patterns. In this universe, it is the movement engendered by reciprocal seductions that brings about the unfolding of life.

Alphonso Lingis, a contemporary philosopher, asks how a world founded upon a dynamic of eroticism would be experienced:

> Could one then imagine an eroticism that would spread every-where, invade all the domains of high culture, and not be a contagion of misery, not be driven by frustration? An eroti-cism that would sensualize the mind in its quest for the truth of the real, that would infect the political order, that would intensify through artifices and in art, and that would be nowhere dissimulated or dissimulating, but discover its climactic intensity in the most sublime forms (1983, 58)?

Lingis finds his answer as it is depicted in the temple carvings of Khajuraho in India:

> ... this abstract geometry embraces within itself layer upon layer of friezes where what seems to be a universal combina-torium of carnal positions is brought to the same explicitness and precision. Auto-erotic stimulation, dual and multiple cunnilinctio, penilinctio, copulation, homosexual and bestial intercourse circulate about the temple walls, without primacy of place or of artistry given to any figure.... Here one neither descends when one makes love with animals and trees, nor ascends when one makes love with the moon, the rivers, the stars; one travels aimlessly or circularly about a universe eroticized (1983, 59, 62).

What Lingis is describing is an eroticized way of seeing and expe-riencing the world, a vision that is not afraid of seduction but

"joins with" the world in a circular, horizontal fashion that cele-
brates the primacy of a multiplicity of perspective imagined as
thousands of sexual positions.

I would like to conclude by suggesting that if we can make the
imaginal leap from seduction as shameful to mutual seduction as
a universal dynamic, then our idea of Jung's notion of individuation and the self will change. The neoplatonic circularity of eros
is echoed in Jung's use of the term "self," as symbolized in the
legendary Echenis fish which "exercises an attraction on ships
that could best be compared with the influence of a magnet on
iron (!). The attraction, so the historical tradition says, emanates
from the fish and brings the vessel, whether powered by sail or
oarsmen, to a standstill" (Jung [1951] 1959c, 9: 154). Here, the
source of the attracting power in the metaphor of fishing is
reversed. It is now the fish that draws out the fisherman![5]

Jung goes on to explain that the alchemists sought to replace
the fish with an instrument that would produce the same effect.
This instrument, the "magnet of the wise," can be taught as a
body of practical knowledge, Jung writes, and he makes the
connection between this secret knowledge, the "real arcanum of
alchemy," and the practice of psychotherapy. Jung connects
extraction with the self:

> In the unconscious are hidden those "sparks of light" *scintil-
> lae*, the archetypes, from which a higher meaning can be
> "extracted" ("extraction of the cogitation"). The "magnet"
> that attracts the hidden thing is the self, or in this case the
> "theoria" or the symbol representing it, which the adept uses
> as an instrument ([1955-56] 1959d, 14: 491).

I would suggest that this sense of the self, as the process
through which essences are extracted, manifests in our daily work
of analysis in the little forms or emanations that make their
appearance through the interaction between analyst and patient
— necessarily seductive because it draws out essences. Here, the
self becomes not a triumphant goal of higher consciousness;
rather the goal is the work itself, as Paracelsus' definition of
alchemy implied, a revealing or evoking of essences through the
seductions and attractions spiraling between patient and therapist. The self would be represented not so much as a sparkling
diamond, numinous globe, or symmetrical geometric figure, but

those odd, waxy, weird aspects of an individual's nature that are led out in the little moments of the analytic hour. Jung wrote:

> The *idiosyncrasy* of an individual is ... to be understood as ... a unique combination, or gradual differentiation, of functions and faculties which in themselves are universal.... Individuation, therefore, can only mean a *process* of psychological development that fulfills the individual qualities given ... it is a process by which a man becomes the definite *unique* being he in fact is ... fulfilling the *peculiarity* of his nature [my emphasis] (1953, 7: 173-74).

With a nod to Yeats, the center is the rough gyration, the slouching turning and turning of Bethlehem and the beast.

Notes

[1] Kerr (1993, 145) shows how Freud's early remarks on the novel *Gradiva* make the devices of seduction equivalent to psychoanalytic technique.

[2] See *The Journal of Analytical Psychology* 40, no.1 (January 1995) for several articles on the nuances of the treatment of trauma.

[3] James Hillman, "Unpublished Notes," "New Mexico Seminar on Alchemy," 1975.

[4] Lorena Bobbitt, the Virginia woman who took a kitchen knife to her soldier husband's penis, might have grabbed the wrong implement. What she really needed was the salt shaker!

[5] Just as the fish, as paradoxically that which is attracted and attracting, is a symbol of the self, so also is Christ as paradoxically fisherman, fish, and bait, a self symbol. He is "fisher of man," as well as alchemically depicted as fishing for Leviathan with the "line of David." Alchemically, he is the fish, as Jung ([1951] 1959c) points out. As well, he can be seen as the "bait," in his descent into limbo, following his death on the cross, which allows for the release of the righteous souls (Kalsched 1981).

Bibliography

Bacon, Roger. 1975. *The Mirror of Alchemy*. Los Angeles: The Globe Bookstore.

Carotenuto, Aldo. 1982. *A Secret Symmetry*. New York: Pantheon Books.

Ellenberger, Henri. 1970. *The Discovery of the Unconscious*. New York:

Basic Books.

Freud, Sigmund. [1914] 1915. "Observations on Transference-love." *Standard Edition of the Complete Psychological Works of Sigmund Freud* 15: 157-71. London: The Hogarth Press.

Hillman, James. 1982. "Salt: A Chapter in Alchemical Psychology." In *Images of the Untouched,* edited by Joanne Stroud and Gail Thomas, 111-37. Dallas: Spring Publications.

Jung, C.G. 1953. "The Relations Between the Ego and the Unconscious." In *Two Essays on Analytical Psychology: Collected Works* 7: 121-241. Princeton, New Jersey: Princeton University Press.

——. 1954. "The Psychology of the Transference." In *The Practice of Psychotherapy: Collected Works* 16: 163-323. Princeton, New Jersey: Princeton University Press.

——. 1959a. "Archetypes of the Collective Unconscious." In *The Archetypes and the Collective Unconscious: Collected Works* 9: 3-41. Princeton, New Jersey: Princeton University Press.

——. [1950] 1959b. "Concerning Mandala Symbolism." In *The Archetypes and the Collective Unconscious: Collected Works* 9: 355-84. Princeton, New Jersey: Princeton University Press.

——. [1951] 1959c. *Aion.* Princeton, New Jersey: Princeton University Press.

——. [1955-56] 1959d. *Mysterium Coniunctionis: Collected Works* 14. Princeton, New Jersey: Princeton University Press.

——. 1965. *Memories, Dreams, Reflections,* recorded and edited by Aniela Jaffe. New York: Random House.

Kalsched, Donald. 1981. "Limbo and the Lost Soul in Psychotherapy." *Union Seminary Quarterly Review* 36: nos. 2 and 3 (Winter/Spring): 95-107.

Kerr, John. 1993. *A Most Dangerous Method.* New York: Knopf.

Lawrence. D.H. 1976. *The Rainbow.* New York: Penguin Books.

Lingis, Alphonso. 1983. *Excesses: Eros and Culture.* Albany, New York: State University of New York Press.

Miller, David. 1981. *Christs: Meditations on Archetypal Images in Christian Theology.* New York: The Seabury Press.

Otto, Rudolf. 1923. *The Idea of the Holy.* London: Oxford University Press.

Plato. 1961a. "Phaedrus." In *The Collected Dialogues of Plato*, edited by Edith Hamilton and Huntington Cairns and translated by R. Hackforth, 475-525. Princeton, New Jersey: Princeton University Press.

——. 1961b. "Symposium." In *The Collected Dialogues of Plato*, edited by Edith Hamilton and Huntington Cairns and translated by R. Hackforth, 526-74. Princeton, New Jersey: Princeton University Press.

Rutter, Peter. 1991. *Sex in the Forbidden Zone*. New York: Fawcett Crest.

Schwartz-Salant, Nathan. 1984. "Archetypal Factors Underlying Sexual Acting Out in the Transference/Countertransference Process." In *Transference/Countertransference*, edited by Nathan Schwartz-Salant and Murray Stein. Wilmette, Illinois: Chiron Publications.

Springer, Anne. 1995. "Paying Homage to the Power of Love." In *The Journal of Analytical Psychology* 40, no. 1.

Waite, Arthur, ed. 1976. *The Hermetic and Alchemical Writings of Paracelsus* 1. Berkeley: Shambala Press.

Chapter 8

The Alchemy of Male Desire: Femininity as Totem and Taboo

Scott D. Churchill

Introduction

An unfortunate perception of male desire predominates in recent discussions regarding the relationship between the sexes. Many have gone to great lengths to emphasize a lack of mutuality (in principle, as well as in practice) when it comes to social interaction between men and women. More alarming is the fact that some feminist authors who see heterosexual scenarios as patriarchically-driven appear to be promoting a view that precludes the female's mutual participation in heterosexual relations. Male behaviors are more and more being perceived by women as offensively intrusive, and this experienced intrusiveness seems, ultimately, to undermine the possibility of reciprocity between men and women. For some, sexism is manifested in even seemingly benign comments, such as those of phenomenologist Maurice Merleau-Ponty, when he suggests that the sexual physiognomy of the female body "elicits" the gestures of the masculine body. To this, Judith Butler protests that the masculine author has, here, "not only projected his own desire onto the female body, but then has accepted that projection as the very structure of the body that he perceives" ([1981] 1989, 93-94).

It is precisely this "projection" that I wish to explore first. It may be difficult, ultimately, to make fine distinctions among projection, identification, perception, and desire. My understanding at the outset is that social and sexual intercourse among human beings, regardless of their biological sex or gender role identifications, is always overdetermined (Freud), overflowing (Sartre), ambiguous (Merleau-Ponty), constituted as much by language as by libido (Lacan), ruled by the archetypal imagination, and alchemically transgressive and complex (Jung). I will show

that it is wrong to assume that male desire necessarily "objecti-
fies" and/or "alienates" the female subject[1] of desire; that, in fact,
an identification with the female (or the one in the female role)
can occur in which this Other is fully vested with subjectivity —
indeed, where the female body and receptive role are taken up
vicariously and sustained with pleasure by the male, while the
female delights in her participation and co-determination of the
encounter. We might tentatively posit that this act of identification on the part of the male participant represents an awakening
of his *anima* — or, more broadly speaking, of his feminine side —
and that such an identification is ultimately in service of male
individuation. I shall also suggest that beneath the veneer of male
arrogance is (sometimes? often?) the fantasy of submission, an
"unconscious" desire to be passive, feminine. The complex play of
unity and differentiation being considered here is understood to be
part of the "alchemy" of the sexes.

I will begin by presenting some depth-psychological formulations on male sexuality, bringing Jung into dialogue first with
Merleau-Ponty's phenomenology, and then with various developmental theories. This will lead to a reflection on male experiences
of desire, with the aim of showing that the male's desire is not
inherently destructive but, quite to the contrary, is capable of
constituting a structure or "complex" that is adoringly apprecia-
tive of the female body. Later, I will discuss feminist attitudes
toward male sexual inadequacy and male effeminacy, which will
lead us to question whether social influence may oppose male
individuation. Finally, I will raise the question of whether there
might be a way out of the patterns of oppression and mutual
condemnation that subtend our current relations among the
sexes.

Depth Psychological Formulations of Male Sexuality

No man is so entirely masculine that he has nothing feminine
in him (Jung [1935] 1953, 189).

The aim of individuation is nothing less than to divest the self
of the false wrappings of the persona on the one hand and the
suggestive power of primordial images on the other (Jung
[1935] 1953, 174).

Jung ([1956] 1970) invokes the *coniunctio oppositorum* (namely, the "union of opposites") as the secret behind the appearance of the feminine in male experience. To understand male desire, Jung directs us to look not only at the "phallic" masculinity that dominates the male ego, but at the feminine archetypes that are inherent in a man's psyche, yet often remain underdeveloped. Jung writes:

> The persona, the ideal picture of a man as he should be, is inwardly compensated by feminine weakness, and as the individual outwardly plays the strong man, so he becomes inwardly a woman, i.e., the anima, for it is the anima that reacts to the persona ([1935] 1953, 194-95).[2]

The last part of this statement merits special consideration, insofar as we shall see below that a man can experience himself at once on "both sides" of a sexual encounter. That is, while performing as the strong (or gentle!) man, he might also find himself consciously or unconsciously identifying with his female partner. Jung offers us a way of accounting for this by suggesting that the identification is born of one's own anima[3] reacting to the surface acts (the "acting-out") of one's persona.

Jung observes: "it is very difficult for a man to distinguish himself from his anima, the more so because she is invisible" ([1928] 1953, 195). To the extent that the anima remains invisibly "behind" a man's gaze as a filter of his experience (rather than being displayed in front of his gaze, like an object that crosses one's path), one might say that it is destined to live on in him "as a manner of being and with a certain degree of generality."[4] Indeed, a man can remain blind to this dimension of himself precisely because of its "generality" — the result of which is that this complex only falls into relief when it is seen "over there" in the presence of another person. In his essay, "Eye and Mind," Merleau-Ponty writes:

> ... my own body's `invisibility' can invest the other bodies that I see. Hence, my body can assume segments derived from the body of another, just as my substance passes into them; man is the mirror for man ([1960] 1964, 168).

The "invisible" anima of which Jung originally spoke leads to a transgressive alchemy that might have been described by

Merleau-Ponty as "a reciprocal insertion and intertwining" of others in us, and of us in them.

Without the other, "I am always on the same side of my body; it presents itself to me in one invariable perspective" (Merleau-Ponty [1964] 1968, 148). With the appearance of the other (especially in a sexual encounter), I discover a "miraculous prolongation of my own intentions" (Merleau-Ponty [1945] 1962, 354) wherein the other's gestures furnish my own intentions with a visible realization — even if I fail to recognize what I contribute to the qualities that I perceive in my partner. Sartre observed: "To love delicate hands is, we might say, a certain way *of loving* these hands *delicately*" ([1940] 1948, 99). The point here is that I bring my own feminine side to my encounter with the female other, just as I bring my own masculine side. (The latter is the source of what is sometimes called "performance anxiety," just as the former is the source of what Freud called "castration anxiety." We shall see later in the essay how performance, castration, and anxiety coalesce in the alchemy of desire.)

Individuation requires that I begin to sort out for myself what I will choose to retain from society's demands of me, as well as what I will choose to retain from the anima's hold on me. Both represent, at least in part, "collective" interests, and it is Jung's contention that we owe it to ourselves to become at least somewhat clear about the differences that exist between our "own" desires and these representatives of collective interests: "I might just as well learn to distinguish between what I want and what the unconscious thrusts upon me, as to see what my office demands of me and what I myself desire" ([1935] 1953, 196). The latter, of course, is something to which we can quite easily relate, namely, the idea of "becoming one's own man" in the face of (and in spite of) social pressures to the contrary. What is of more interest here is the former issue, pertaining to the tension between desires of the ego and the sometimes ego-dystonic desires of the anima. Jung observes:

> So long as the anima is unconscious she is always projected, for everything unconscious is projected. The first bearer of the soul-image is always the mother; later it is borne by those women who arouse the man's feelings, whether in a positive or a negative sense. The safeguard against the unconscious,

> which is what his mother meant to him, is not replaced by anything in the modern man's education; unconsciously, therefore ... under the cloak of the ideally exclusive marriage he is really seeking his mother's protection (Jung [1935] 1953, 197-98).

The challenge for the man is to become at least partially conscious of his anima so that it will not have to exist solely in "the Other," whether that be in the form of an unconscious projection or in the form of a person who replaces the social role of one's mother.

In his discussion of Jung's notion of individuation, analyst Eugene Monick comments that "when the mid-life crisis attacks, the baby part of the man is unmasked as a factor in the adult personality, often with striking clarity" (1991, 33). This infantile dimension calls out for maternal attention at the same time that it effects a "transformation" of the male psyche in which the male once again experiences no differentiation between his body and his mother/partner's:

> Individuation is not the repair of an earlier failure ... [rather, it] requires a turning into, rather than away from, precisely what has heretofore been avoided: the subjective feminine, the antithesis of phallic manifestation and prowess (Monick 1991, 34).

Thus, individuation allows a man to achieve a wholeness which "includes a man's subjective inclusion of the feminine, the contra-sexual opposite, not in another person but in himself" (Monick 1991, 34). It turns out, however, that what is precisely "forbidden" to men in our culture is a feminine identification that would threaten the lingering phallocentrism of male adolescence:

> Individuation for a man has to do with his willingness to embrace in himself what, from a patriarchal perspective, seems like weakness and castration....
>
> Individuation for a man is when he begins to know that phallos is only half of the fabric of life, and that he has the image of the other half within. It behooves a man to get to know that other half in preparation for a winding down, a softer time, a return to the mother (Monick 1991, 35).

Issues pertaining to the male's acting-out of the anima will be addressed later in the essay. Long before any "winding down," however, this feminine "other half" is an activating force within burgeoning male desire.

The Forbidden Anima in Male Individuation

The feminine shows itself, curiously enough, in what is both reviled by and fascinating to, (the boy within) the man. For example, the peer-influenced fear of "cooties" during the juvenile era of many male baby-boomers (both maintained and assuaged by the group ritual of morning "cootie shots" in school classrooms) might eventually have led to the breeding of unnecessary attitudes of misogyny in adulthood. But this is only a superficial illustration of a much deeper issue pertaining to something within man himself that assails him. At least during pre-adolescent "latency," the boy consciously (albeit secretly) harbors the truth that he is enthralled with his female counterparts. The problem begins in adolescence when reflective intellectual powers come into play (Piaget's "formal operations") and young men begin to think they need to isolate (and thus preserve) their own masculinity by banishing the feminine from their own direct experience. The male adolescent's "anima" remains "over there," at a safe distance, and, lest he be tempted to take it up and assume it within his own experience and manners of expression, he joins with other adolescent males in rituals of verbal degradation ("locker room talk") by which the feminine becomes established as a kind of taboo that remains off-limits unless there is some kind of triumph involved in one's relationship to it. (This would also seem to lie at the basis of male homophobia: an aversion to the manifestation of the feminine in another male — which means, an aversion to the male who, rather than triumphing over his feminine side, gives full expression to it.[5]) It is important to note that while "feminine" and "female" may represent distinct categories for the psychologist, they can become conflated in the experience of the adolescent male as a result of a "projection" that enables him to be fully conscious of the feminine but only insofar as it exists apart from himself (as well as from other men[6]).

Soon after puberty, the sex act gets languaged and anticipated as a drama of conquering the female (and thus both possessing and taming the feminine within oneself). The inability of adolescent (and many adult) males to experience and talk about a balance of the masculine and feminine within themselves can thus be traced to an earlier emotional ambivalence regarding the integration of opposing feelings toward the self and others. Specifically, as revealed to us by the object-relations school of analysis, the challenge of integrating the "good mother" with the "bad mother" (and, correlatively, the "good me" and "bad me") during early childhood sets the stage for the resolution of all subsequent oppositions.[7] If "the rigid child tends to project outside himself the part of himself he does not want to be" (Merleau-Ponty [1960] 1964, 103), then it is important to look at the images of others rejected in childhood in order to discover the aspects of the self that are destined to become problematic in subsequent individuation. Intellectual attitudes eventually follow from early emotional experiences, and it is thus that Merleau-Ponty writes:

> The more emotionally ambivalent the subject, the less it suits him that there should be any ambiguity in things and in his view of things. Emotional ambivalence is what demands the denial of intellectual ambiguity (Merleau-Ponty [1960] 1964, 105).

If ambiguity characterizes the normal state of adaptivity wherein the individual is comfortable with his psychic "counterparts," it must be recognized that such a state represents the achievement of adulthood, which is a developmental stage that does not come simply with age. While not all men experience their feminine sides split-off from themselves, it does appear to be a normal part of development for males to be at least somewhat ambivalent about their feminine inclinations. Alfred Adler characterized this ambivalence as "the masculine protest. It follows necessarily as over-compensation when the 'feminine' tendency is valued negatively by the childish judgment" ([1910] 1978, 36).[8] Such over-compensation sometimes takes extreme forms, as in the case of those individuals whose gender identity becomes totalized on the masculine side. This tendency can be seen in "phallic-narcissistic" males, as well as in certain homosexual females. Erik Erikson later suggested that the young people of our time have become "ready to support doctrines offering a total immersion in a synthetic identity," and are quick to collaborate in a "collective condemnation of a totally stereotyped enemy of the new identity"

(1968, 89). The male whose intellectual "synthesis" of a masculine ideal precludes any trace of the feminine thus eagerly adjoins
himself to talk that safeguards his "new" (and ambivalent) identity. Erikson called this attitude "totalism" and considered it a
part of "normal psychology":

> [It] evokes a Gestalt in which absolute boundary is empha-
> sized: given a certain arbitrary delineation, nothing that
> belongs inside must be left outside, nothing that must be
> outside can be tolerated inside. A totality is as absolutely
> inclusive as it is utterly exclusive (1968, 81).

It was precisely during developmental shifts and upheavals that a
man "restructures himself and the world by taking recourse to
what we may call *totalism*" (Erikson 1968, 81).

It is important to note that this totalism of the masculine
during male adolescence (with its concomitant totemism of the
phallus) does not succeed in eliminating the feminine from male
sexuality; it only removes it to a safer distance in the form of a
"shadow." One experience in which the male is able to come face
to face (and flesh to flesh) with the feminine is in the sexual
encounter with a female. More specifically, there are sexual
"games" played by mutually consenting adults in which scenarios
are enacted that allow each participant to explore his or her
psychic counterpart within the safety of proscribed limits. When
fantasies of dominance and submission are thus played out
between consenting adults, we have an opportunity to observe the
erotic imagination unleashed from its typical constraints. Such a
situation is ideal for studying gender role identifications at both
conscious and unconscious levels.

Male (Desire for) Identification with the Female Body

In a recent study (Churchill 1993), I examined male experiences of
desire and focussed upon a unique experience where a male
subject fantasized what it would be like to experience what his
female partner was experiencing. Such a fantasy would be fascinating to explore even when it remained entirely within the realm
of the imaginary; however, this scenario blossoms into a fully
carnal act of identification when it is lived out in actual sexual
encounter. One case involved a man and a woman playing a game

of bondage in which the woman asked to be blindfolded with her hands tied above her head, while her partner played out a scenario in which she was his captive. The man describing this experience revealed himself to be profoundly connected to his partner's body, touching its surface very gently with his own body, but feeling more what he imagined to be the sensations in her body, than those in his own. The following is an excerpt from that description:

> The experience that comes to mind is not a "typical" experience, by any means.... Anyway, my girlfriend wanted me to tie her hands together with her nylons and make her submit to my sexual demands. I was excited by this at first, but underneath I had reservations, because I had never really thought about actually doing that to somebody. It wasn't really my style to be aggressive — sexually or otherwise — and I was almost afraid of feeling silly actually pretending to dominate her sexually.... The moment she was blindfolded I told her to stretch her arms over her head ... she gasped lightly, and I immediately felt aroused and less self-conscious about what was going on. It was as if I were the one gasping at the excitement of what was to come. From that point on I felt like I was performing a script that was vaguely familiar to me, even though I'd never really done this before.... I proceeded to explore her body, very gently stroking here and there.... It was very exciting. A kind of "pure" sexual moment — even though I was the one who was in control, it was like I was watching this happen and I was aware of a profound sense of trust and pleasure on her part....
>
> I became totally involved in imagining what might be a pleasurable sensation for her — what would it be like to be spread out like that, submitting to my touch.... I was fascinated by the thought of what it would be like to be in her position.... It's interesting, now that I think about it, that I felt more sexual pleasure in my own body when I was "feeling" her being stroked. Feeling her from the inside out in my imagination — being her body, I guess — that was exciting....
>
> Weeks later she told me "it was the most beautiful sexual arousal I ever experienced."

A traditional psychoanalytic perspective might explain a man's identification in such a situation along the following lines: To escape from what might have been a guilt-ridden conflict arising in adolescence from aggressive sexual fantasies directed toward females, the male identifies with the central figure of his early adolescent fantasies: the innocent girl. In doing so, he disengages himself (if only momentarily) from his active role in playing out the bondage fantasy, as his consciousness begins to inhabit the body of his submissive partner (whom we must recall initiated the fantasy).[9] We might even look further back developmentally to his earliest experience of the Other, namely, the maternal female. Rubin (1983), following both Chodorow (1978) and Dinnerstein (1976), offers the following understanding of male desire drawn from the object-relations school of analysis:

> From the beginning, life is a process of forming attachments, internalizing representations from the external world, and making identifications....
>
> Because a woman has been the primary person in the life of the child until this time, it is with her that this first identification is made. Hers is the imagery that is internalized [my emphasis].... What this says, then, is that, whether in a girl or a boy, the earliest, most primitive experiences of both attachment and identification are with a woman (Rubin 1983, 49, 50).

To identify with a female body during adult sex would thus be to awaken the archaic memory of one's undifferentiated perception of the Mother/Infant Body.

The question we must ponder here has to do with the earlier process of "internalization": is it the incorporation of something that is "not me" into a primitive sense of "me," or is it a primitive representation to myself of the undifferentiated unity that I experience during the stage of symbiosis prior to the event that orthodox analysts call "ego differentiation"? The Jungian answer to this question advances our understanding of male desire, insofar as it states that the anima is not entirely an internalized representation of a present or past perception, but rather an awareness of our phylogenetically-constituted being that is with us from the start. The Jungian understanding allows us to see the male opening himself to his own depths (including both a personal and collective unconscious), and not simply responding to a surface that presents itself from afar. Monick observes:

> In a similar way, a female figure in a man's dream "is" the dreamer's anima. By emotionally connecting with the figure, a dreaming man can begin to know a part of himself which the ego might not accept were it offered straightforwardly, in a declarative manner. Here is where a knowledge of Jung's work is critical. He adds an essential archetypal dimension to Freud's concrete and personal-historical view of male identification with an longing for "mother."
>
> The message from Jung ... is that men must bring themselves to recognize and accept a hidden and terrifying part of themselves (1991, 62-63, 64).

By distinguishing both the libido and the collective unconscious from the personal unconscious, Jung shows us that there are dimensions of sexuality more archaic than our own personal past; hence, a man's anima is not reducible to his earliest introjections of a maternal figure. In recognizing that the male sexual "persona" represents a compromise between the individual personality and the collective psyche, Jung's approach to sexuality thus adds a dimension to our understanding of male desire beyond that found in the object-relations theory.

Returning to the scenario in which the male fantasizes the female's experience, it appears that in order to facilitate a "strong vicarious entering into the feelings of the real partner," the male research subject actively provoked sexual excitement in his partner. Without this, his perception of her pleasure would have been merely a projection; the fact that the male here facilitates sexual pleasure in his partner is a clue to his ultimate identification with her.[10] By thus provoking a willfully submissive female partner to be sexually excited, the male facilitates the precise experience that he will, in turn, enjoy vicariously: guilt-free passivity. His consciousness does not inhabit the aggressive act of touching so much as it dwells in the ecstasy of the body-subject being touched.[11]

Even when "force" becomes a part of the real or imaginary dimensions of a sexual encounter, it is important to note that the actual or fantasized coercion can function as an excuse for one to have sex. Here, it is not necessary to differentiate between the one dominating and the one dominated since this entire scenario originates in the fantasy of the "dominator" precisely so that he can identify with his dominated partner, who becomes, in effect, an alter ego. The roles are interchangeable in such a way to allow a vicarious alteration to take place.[12]

The situation of "having" to submit to sex at the surface functions to remove responsibility and, henceforth, to eliminate the very guilt that psychoanalysts posit as one of the underlying (Oedipal) origins of perversion. However, beneath the "reason" is a secret willingness — indeed, a passionate desire — to engage in sex; and, in fact, it is a secret desire to engage in sex under the seemingly contradictory (because of the choice involved) circumstance of submission.[13] The very fact that the partner is provoked into obvious excitement within the circumstance of the domination/submission scenario is proof of his or her complicity — even though the scenario proceeds with a collusion on the part of both participants to act out their respective roles more or less convincingly.[14]

The sexual strategy is thus a kind of magical act in which we place ourselves under our own spell. (This would be another meaning of my use of the term "alchemy" in the title of this essay.) In his book on *The Emotions*, Sartre writes:

> ... consciousness does not limit itself to projecting affective signification upon the world around it. It *lives* the new world which it has just established.... it endures the qualities which behavior has set up" ([1939] 1948, 75).

Elsewhere, Sartre has written:

> This is why man is always a sorcerer for man. Indeed, this poetic connection of two passivities in which one creates the other spontaneously is the very foundation of ... "participation."
>
> The ego which produces undergoes the reverberation of what it produces. The ego is "compromised" by what it produces. Here a relation reverses itself.... The ego is in some way spellbound by this action, it "participates" with it. Thus everything that the ego produces affects it. We must add: and only what it produces ([1936] 1957, 82).

This helps us to understand how it is that sexual scenarios involving fantasies of dominance and submission break down precisely when one partner cannot perform or "play" his role, even if he can secretly identify with it. Thus, we are able to better understand the intentionality of a vicarious[15] experience in which one desires and identifies with the other's role, and we can begin to appreciate the utter complexity that is involved in even the most basic sexual scenarios.

Already, we have established the sexual scenario and a drama in which one performs a role that is complicated by its origins in one's own desire, even as it comes into play with the expectations of others. Indeed, it is in human conduct itself, in the performance of one's sexuality, that one takes the very risks that enable oneself to individuate. Earlier, we saw that for Jung, in order for a man to become whole,

> ... there is no substitute for an embrace, within himself, of his opposite, his own femininity, his softness, his relatedness — in a sense, his phallic defeat.... [Moreover,] for a man to grow old well, he must accept the need for this last transformation within himself, a reversal of projection of his feminine upon the women in his life (Monick 1991, 65).

The next section of this essay examines ways in which men sometimes find themselves thwarted when attempting to appropriate the feminine within themselves.

The Disparagement of Effeminacy

> An inherited collective image of woman exists in a man's unconscious, with the help of which he apprehends the nature of woman (Jung [1935] 1953, 190).

> Transgressivity, the crossing of boundaries, is a characteristic of the psychoid nature of the archetype and surely related to transformation (Monick 1991, 19).

Within our current "phallocentric" society, there is a noticeable attitude of contempt toward manifestation of the feminine within male behavior (whether in fantasy or in conduct) — an attitude that appears to stand in the way of the kind of liberating personal individuation of which Jung has spoken. We might even say that there is a curious phallocentrism at play in feminists' disparagement of men either who are weak "passive types" or who choose to act out their feminine longings. It is interesting, and perhaps ironic, that we find nowhere a more disparaging and belittling attitude toward passivity in general, and men's secret "feminine" longings in particular, than in the feminist literature. Where one might expect that women would be at least sympathetic, if not supportive, with regard to men with such affinities, we often find instead derisive and emasculating remarks.

In an article on men "performing" as women, Anne Herrmann (1991) makes reference to Billy Wilder's (1959) film, *Some Like It Hot*, in which Tony Curtis and Jack Lemmon play two musicians who join an all-female band while hiding from the mob. Referring to Joe E. Brown's character Osgood Fielding, the billionaire attracted to Lemmon's character Daphne, Herrmann writes: "Effeminacy approaches homosexuality ... [in] Osgood, an older man who wears a bow tie and seems to be looking for a wife to replace his mother" (1991, 187). Although this is not really "offensive" per se, the reference to the bow tie does suggest the image of a little boy, as well as a restrained or even non-existent male sex drive. Osgood is just another mama's boy, a dandy who, for portraying the politically incorrect image of feminine passivity, is made fun of by a female author, who would presumably be more understanding if she were talking about a woman's proclivity for dressing like a "tomboy."

Herrmann's remarks are echoed by Louise Kaplan, who in her book, *Female Perversions*, discusses the case of Mr. K, who happens to be an apron fetishist:

> Undoubtedly, the less controllable spontaneous "leaking out" of the ejaculate and the inevitable detumescence would unconsciously signify, especially to a conventional, rigid man like Mr. K, a realization of his unconscious feminine wishes and therefore terrify him....
>
> ... Though he grew to physical manhood, the sad and tragic conclusion was that Mr. K could only impersonate a man and even that only while safely tied to his mother's apron strings, which is where he would remain eternally (1991, 163, 166).

Kaplan's tone soon changes to sarcasm and then contempt, as she describes another case of male fetishism:

> [George] was never able to penetrate his wife. After several

months of repeated failed coitus, he had the idea [of a shoe fetish] ... that eventually became his sole means of achieving erections and ejaculations. That night he managed to penetrate his wife and to remain erect for nearly two minutes (1991, 135).

A "real man," of course, would not have to "manage" to penetrate his wife — nor would he have any difficulty "remaining erect." Indeed, according to the implicit standard for male sexual performance set by this female psychoanalyst, the expected norm would be *homo phallos:* man-the-always-erect-penetrator. Anything less would be a poor, flaccid substitute for masculinity.[16]

The feminist-psychoanalytic assault on male inadequacy is expressed very clearly when Kaplan later explains:

... [the] passive attitude on the part of a man is the outcome of his sadistic-vengeful attitudes toward females. Many of these men seem to be characteristically lethargic, lacking in energy and masculine get-up-and-go. They strike the observer as decidedly unmanly.... In the more lethargic, passive types, the underlying violence has been counteracted by the opposite character trait — cowardice. In their dreams these same cowardly men very often express the fantasy of killing the woman by copulating with her. The cowardly premature ejaculator does not murder his sexual partner.... They only murder her sexual pleasure (1991, 177).

Throughout her text, Kaplan repeatedly refers to men's "secret feminine longings" as terrifying to them. The irony is in her describing these male desires as "longings," implying an enviable quality in being female — and then repeatedly hammering in the point that such qualities must necessarily be frightening to any man, who is then denounced as less than a man (and thereby more female?) because of this very fear!

It is noteworthy that both Kaplan and Herrmann celebrate females who adopt stereotypically masculine identities. A brief digression from our theme of male desire will suffice to help the reader understand why I consider this to be of interest here. Herrmann's article begins with an almost admiring description of women "passing" as male musicians and bullfighters. Kaplan, following Joan Riviere (1929), characterizes conventional women as pathologically "masquerading" in their stereotypical roles. On the other hand, Kaplan describes both frigid and perverted females, as well as unconventional women whose sexuality and gender identifications are more ambiguous, in sympathetic and even laudatory terms:

> Women who conform to gender stereotypes are women who have been arrested at a pre-stage of gender identity. On the other hand, a female whose femininity is arrived at through a series of solving and resolving the inevitable conflicts of being human is an interesting, dynamic, and complicated woman who is capable of evoking in herself the masculinity *and* femininity of her father or the femininity and masculinity of her mother and arranging and rearranging who she is and what she wants out of life until the day she dies (1991, 190).

Thus, frigidity, Kaplan observes, is "about the anxiety of exhibiting active sexual desire in a social order that forbids these desires to `nice' women" (1991, 180). Similarly, Kaplan is completely sympathetic to the female with masculine strivings, as expressed in this generalization that she makes regarding the personal history of female perverts:

> When she arrives at puberty, if she has not already abandoned, buried, and forgotten her active sexual strivings and intellectual ambitions, she must relinquish them before she becomes an adult woman, or she must disguise them sufficiently so that no one will be the wiser. Indeed ... a not uncommon female perverse scenario entails a masquerade of denigrated, submissive femininity that hides a woman's forbidden and dangerous "masculine" ambitions (1991, 184).

What is different in the feminist treatment of male and female perversions is that the male's feminine longings are described as terrifying to him, while the female's masculine ambitions are dangerous not to herself, but to a patriarchically-driven society. In both cases, it is men who are afraid; and in both, the fear is of the female. The woman plays the martyr in either case. There is a decided imbalance in these female authors' portrayals of perversions and a clear subtext of disdain toward men (but not toward masculinity!).

It seems as though these authors believe that men ought to be active, "manly," and potent; otherwise, there would not be such a mocking tone in their characterization of men who fail to live up to this ideal. On the one hand, when men have the audacity of responding to what they experience as desirable in the female, they are reprimanded for "thinking with their dicks";[17] on the other hand, when they fail to satisfy their partner, or worse, want to dress up in her clothes, they are castigated for not being "man enough."

Conclusion

We have seen by way of Jung that when the anima remains unconscious, she exists for the man in the form of projections that can potentially distort his interpersonal relations, while keeping him blind to a rich inner source of meaning.[18] More specifically, we have seen how the presence of the Other makes possible the awakening in one's own experience of the personal as well as pre-personal (or collective) unconscious figures that otherwise remain closed off from our waking life. I showed, in the first part of the essay, how it can be wrong to generalize about the nature of male desire. We have observed the complex play of masculine and feminine identifications within male experience and have examined some situations where superficial expressions of *phallos* (in the form of sado-masochistic and even homophobic behaviors) belie an underlying ambivalence toward the feminine side of male experience. We have also seen how unconscious dimensions of ourselves become filters of our experience, and how male individuation serves to bring some of these "filters" out into the open.

Moreover, we have also looked at ways that women sometimes participate in the suppression of male expressions of their feminine side, thus encouraging the very phallocentrism (and phallic-intrusive behaviors) that, in the end, will be charged with the oppression of women. It appears that both men and women are ruled by distorting projections that constitute the "lenses" through which we, as adults, reflect and refract each other's presence.

This concluding section, which serves more as an epilogue, examines more closely the psychological and existential polarities that seem to get turned into dangerous oppositions. I will then reflect on some ambiguities of our gendered life that contribute to conflict, and I will suggest a way of moving toward a better sense of mutual reciprocity in our interpersonal relations.

In his book, *Healing Fiction*, James Hillman observes:

> The mind sets up opposite poles: strong/weak, up/down, male/female — and these guiding *fictions* determine how we experience.
>
> ... For [Adler], to think that abstract opposites reflect reality is to think neurotically, since all antitheses ultimately refer to the power construct of superior/inferior embodied in society as male and female (1983, 100).

Feminists have defined "phallocentrism" as a binary signifying system that assumes dichotomies in general and heterosexuality in particular. The phallogocentric establishment has allegedly opposed male presence to female absence, a male center to the female margin, the active male to the inert female, a positive definition of masculinity to an either neutral or negative definition of femininity, the male master to the female slave, male desire to female embodiment, and the male word principle to the female verbal object (see Shaktini 1989).

In contrast, depth psychologists in the Jungian tradition paint a more balanced picture of the male and female, and of masculine and feminine dimensions of the psyche. Hillman, in fact, draws upon Adler to present a view of sexuality that sees the masculine and feminine not as "opposites," but as sedimentary elements within the common soil of the psyche:

> Antitheses divide the world sharply, giving opportunity for exerting power in forceful actions, saving us from feeling weak and incapacitated. More important even than these pairs is that oppositional thinking itself is a pampering safeguard against the true reality of the world, which in Adler's view is one of shaded differentiations and not oppositions (Hillman 1983, 100).

If Adler's notion of "shaded differentiation" can be amplified to indicate the presence of one's "shadow" within the adumbrations of one's sexuality, and if we heal the oppositional thinking characteristic of contemporary intellectual discussions by acknowledging the fundamental ambiguity of both our "inner" sense of identity and our more outward self-expressions, then we can begin to see more clearly the way that psyche is infused with confluent

desires, creating alchemical contexts within which we are sometimes thrown into confusion and conflict.

The ambiguity of mutuality versus conflict in sexual experiences can be grasped perhaps most simply in terms of what Laing
(1967) has called "interexperience" — consisting here of my
desire, my experience of your desire, my experience of your experience of my desire, and so on. This whole scenario is, however,
complicated once we acknowledge the shadow-play in which we
have my conscious and unconscious desires, my conscious as well
as unconscious experience of your conscious and unconscious
desires, and so on.

Mutuality occurs when one experiences the "for-me" of the
other's desire, as well as the "for-the-other" of one's own desire.
Conflict occurs when one or both individuals are, to some degree,
estranged or even alienated from the other's center of subjectivity,
caught up in a solipsistic frame of reference. One of my concerns
has been that in the feminist critique of male desire as just a
carnal form of misogyny, we find the symptom of a conflict that
has two sides to it. On the one hand, there is the way one experiences the Other's regard for oneself; on the other hand, there is the
stance one takes in response to this perception. The first side of
the conflict is the experience of a gender oppression that "objecti-
fies, marginalizes, and silences women" (Allen and Young 1989,
16). The other side of the dilemma resides in the stance taken by
some women toward the phallocentric Other by whom they experience themselves as neglected. Sartre ([1943] 1956) has described
such a stance as one of hatred. It exists in concrete relations with
others when one experiences oneself as objectified by the Other,
when one feels shame or fear in the face of the Other's gaze.

Notice that it is not a question of establishing how the other
"actually" comports himself or herself toward us, but rather of
grasping and understanding how we "experience" his or her
comportment: What is of phenomenological interest is how the
other appears to us.[19] It is my contention that this appearance is
a function not only of how the other is actually acting at the
moment, but of one's fundamental relation towards others, which
is itself a function of both the history of one's perceptions of how
others regard oneself and the alchemy of heterosexual desire. This
fundamental relation of the male to the female acts as a "horizon"

of my perception of others, coloring each of my encounters with people whom I meet; furthermore, it is an attitude that is at least to some extent chosen by me.

If one's experience of a sexual encounter is as much a function of one's own attitudes and perceptions as it is of the other's actual comportment toward oneself, then we might consider working back to these attitudes and to the experiences that serve as their origin. On either or both sides of a sexual relationship, we are likely to find someone projecting one's own ends to the exclusion of the other's, thus finding the presence of another's needs or subjectivity in general to be a bothersome obstacle to be passed over. In such cases, even the invitation to participate in a mutually reciprocal relationship can become problematic.

What is generally needed, I think, is a better sense of empathy for each other's position: a more benevolent, more generous interpretation of the other's desires. If we choose not to close ourselves off individually or collectively from genuine engagement with the Other, then we ought to examine our modes of presence to each other that constitute the habitual, socially constructed, politically motivated perceptions that are currently placing a wall of fear and hatred between men and women. If the move from the unconscious to the conscious is made by means of speech, then perhaps we need to listen more carefully to each other, if we are to transcend the limiting biases and confused awakenings of our earlier experiences. To quote Derrida,

> ... everything comes down to the ear you are able to hear me with" (1985, 4).

Notes

1 By "subject," I mean to acknowledge the female as an agent, and not just an object in the interpersonal field — as one "for whom," and not just "by means of which," a sexual drama unfolds. At the same time, the term "subject" is intended here to connote ambiguously the nominative agent of desire who is nonetheless subject(ed) to another's desire.

2 Jung writes:

> This arbitrary segment of collective psyche — often fashioned with considerable pains — I have called the *persona*. The term *persona* is really a very appropriate expression for this, for originally it meant the mask worn by actors to indicate the role they played.... It is, as

its name implies, only a mask of the collective psyche, a mask that *feigns individuality* ... whereas one is simply acting a role through which the collective psyche speaks.... Fundamentally the persona is nothing real: It is a compromise between individual and society as to what a man should appear to be ([1935] 1953, 157-58).

3 Jung uses the term "anima" as a transgressive and universal construct — a structure that goes beyond the idiosyncratic subjectivity of male desire by tapping into the collective psyche.

4 I borrow this phrase from Merleau-Ponty ([1945] 1962, 83), who uses it in reference to the phenomenon of fixation (see note 7 below).

5 At the same time, homophobia represents an aversion to the feminine side of oneself that responds, even if unconsciously, to the sexual invitation of another male who appears to be "gay."

6 The curious concern that some males have of prohibiting the expression of the feminine by other males is evidenced by those late-night talk show audience members who protest vigorously when transvestites and "pre-op transsexuals" flaunt their femininity in the audience members' faces. Interestingly, aggressive homophobic responses might be viewed as explicit efforts on the part of these individuals to passionately engage themselves face-to-face with another man whose female identification is conveniently up-front (and thus more available than the viewer's own repressed femininity), thereby facilitating a kind of vicarious mirroring of the other in one's own being. On a recent Jerry Springer show, one male audience member burst up to the microphone and threatened to a female impersonator seated on stage that if she twirled her pigtail just one more time, he was going to "personally shove it up [her] ass." (The explicit aggression of such an act would appear to an analyst as a counter-phobic measure to conceal the underlying homoeroticism suggested by the audience member's overwrought interest in the panelist, and especially by his aggression toward the panelist's "tail"!)

7 Referring to the work of Else Frenkel-Brunswik and Melanie Klein, Merleau-Ponty remarked that, "ambivalence consists in having two alternative images of the same object, the same person, without making any effort to connect them or to notice that in reality they relate to the same object and the same person" ([1960] 1964, 102-03). Merleau-Ponty continues: "Ambiguity is ambivalence that one dares to look at face to face. What is lacking in rigid subjects in this capacity to confront squarely the contradictions that exist in their attitudes toward others" ([1960] 1964,

103). For Klein, ambivalence amounts to a kind of psychic splitting, whereby what is deemed good is maintained in consciousness, while what is deemed bad is expelled to the outer world. However, it would be more truthful to say, as Merleau-Ponty says of repression in general, that what is denied within oneself, "does not leave us but remains constantly hidden behind our gaze ... as a manner of being" ([1945] 1962, 83). It is precisely this "manner of being" that remains veiled from our perception of ourselves (though not from our perception of others) — and that, among other things, comprises a man's *anima*.

8 In *Analysis Terminable and Interminable*, Freud observes:
> Something which both sexes have in common has been forced, by the difference between the sexes, into different forms of expressions. The two corresponding themes are in the female, an *envy for the penis* ... and, in the male, a struggle against his passive or feminine attitude to another male. What is common to the two themes was singled out at an early date by psycho-analytic nomenclature as an attitude towards the castration complex. Subsequently Alfred Adler brought the term "masculine protest" into current use. It fits the case of males perfectly; but I think that, from the start, "repudiation of femininity" would have been the correct description of this remarkable feature in the psychical life of human beings.... [I]n both cases it is the attitude proper to the opposite sex which has succumbed to repression ([1937] 1964, 250-51).

One can read Freud's statement above in the following way: that what the male represses is the feminine way of repudiating the feminine, namely, through penis envy. Whereas the female makes out of the phallus a totem, the male would experience (his own) feminine longing for the phallus as taboo, insofar as it would awaken in himself an uncomfortable feeling of homoeroticism. Thus, for example, the image of the voluptuous female masturbating in Picasso's painting, "The Dream," becomes a totem for the male at a conscious level, while her own totemism of the phallus (her desire to give herself over to the phallus) — which would be the ultimate Oedipal meaning of her femininity — remains as off limits to the male as it is unconscious to the waking consciousness of the dreaming figure in the painting.

9 It is important to acknowledge that we are focusing here on a particular situation where both male and female participate as agents (where the role of the "agent" or sexual "subject" includes inventing the sexual drama, enacting it, and feeling the pleasure of its realization). In such circumstances where both male and female are indeed participating as subjects, identification with one's partner is going to be more than a

primitive projection, insofar as each person both preserves and enjoys the other's being.

10 The importance of this distinction will become more apparent in note 17 below, where we examine a feminist critique of Merleau-Ponty's phenomenology of desire.

11 We must remember that we are examining the situation here from only one side of the encounter. Thus, we are suspending interest in the question of power, as well as the question of whether his experience is congruent with hers. However, Simone de Beauvoir has an interesting way of considering both sides of such an encounter — one that does not conflate projective identification with hostility:

> Some women say that they feel the masculine sex organ in them as a part of their own bodies; some men feel that they *are* the women they penetrate. These are evidently inexact expressions, for the dimension, the relation of the *other* still exists; but the fact is that alterity has no longer a hostile implication, and indeed this sense of the union of really separate bodies is what gives its emotional character to the sexual act; and it is the more overwhelming as the two beings, who together in passion deny and assert their boundaries, are similar and yet unlike ([1949] 1989, 401).

12 The motivation behind such vicarious experience might best be explained by Freud:

> The matter is made more difficult to grasp by the complicating circumstances that even in boys the Oedipus complex has a double orientation, active and passive, in accordance with their bisexual constitution; a boy also wants to take his mother's place as the love-object of his father — a fact which we describe as the feminine attitude" ([1925] 1990, 307).

The concept of "castration anxiety" enters the scene at this point and takes the male in two conflicting directions: he can retreat into feminine fantasies, but then fear ostracism/castration because of them. What currently is being talked about as "homophobia" in heterosexual, as well as latent homosexual, men is a function of just this very form of castration anxiety. "The male, who does not have a `masculine' and a `feminine' genital zone [as does the woman with her clitoris and vagina, respectively], who does not change zones, does not repress his femininity in a comparable way [to how women repress their masculinity]" (Bruehl-Young 1990, 24).

13 Although feminists have made compelling arguments against such a

position when it concerns the psychology of female experience, I am here basing my understanding on the data of male fantasy with regard to submissive scenarios in which the male identifies with the one in the submissive role. Women, including feminists, have affirmed to me through personal testimony the eroticism of submission as characterized here (even if some have felt compelled to acknowledge the political "incorrectness" of such affirmation).

14 As in any fetish or ritual, the performance has to be convincing enough to fulfill the self-deceptive needs of the performers. As Robert Stoller (1985) observed, "We experience a moment of excitement ... as spontaneously and instantaneously produced, as if we played no part in its creation" (22). And yet, we are indeed performing roles that we choose, all the while pretending otherwise. (See, especially, Wanda von Sacher-Masoch's [1907/1970] fascinating recollections of her husband's wish to be a slave.) Identification with the one in the role reciprocal to ourselves is one way of pretending not to be choosing the role one is playing at the moment. This works both ways and in socially constructed gender-preferential modes: where the dominated female identifies with her dominator, and the dominating male identifies with the women he dominates. As we shall see later, both are fleeing from the "socially determined" gender identities that evoke a sense of shame in the face of their secret longings.

15 I use the term, "vicarious," here to imply an experience that is both "other" (insofar as it appears to originate outside of myself in the other's body), and, at the same time, touching upon something structural within myself.

16 Is this not in essence, however, the same charge made by feminists about male expectations of women — namely, that women are egregiously expected by males to be always ready and willing to have sex?

17 An interesting case in point is the one referred to at the outset of this essay, regarding Merleau-Ponty's phenomenology of sexuality. In his *Phenomenology of Perception*, Merleau-Ponty writes:

> In the case of the normal subject, a body is not perceived merely as an object; this objective perception has within it a more intimate perception: the visible body is subtended by a sexual schema which is strictly individual, emphasizing the erogenous areas, outlining a sexual physiognomy, and eliciting the gestures of the masculine body which is itself integrated into this emotional totality ([1945] 1962, 156).

Now, let us look at what Judith Butler wrote (early in her career) regarding this passage:

> Viewed as an expression of sexual ideology, *The Phenomenology of Perception* reveals the cultural construction of the masculine subject as a *strangely disembodied* voyeur whose sexuality is *strangely noncorporeal....* Erotic experience is almost never described as tactile or physical or even passionate.... *As Merleau-Ponty notes, the schema subtending the body emphasizes the erogenous zones, but it remains unclear whether the "erogenous areas" are erogenous to the perceiving subject or to the subject perceived. Perhaps ... it is of no consequence (to Merleau-Ponty) whether the experience is shared by the subject perceived.... Moreover, the sexual physiognomy of the female body "elicit[s] the gestures of the masculine body," as if the very existence of these attributes "provoked" or even necessitated certain kinds of sexual gestures on the part of the male. Here it seems that the masculine subject has not only projected his own desire onto the female body, but then has accepted that projection as the very structure of the body that he perceives. Here the solipsistic circle of the masculine voyeur seems complete (Butler [1981] 1989, 93-94 [emphasis added to indicate the incongruence between Butler's characterization of Merleau-Ponty and the latter's own statements]).

Butler concludes that for Merleau-Ponty, "female bodies appear to have an essence which is itself physical," thereby designating the female body "as an object rather than a subject of perception" (Butler [1981] 1989, 94), and thus revealing a "misogyny" at the heart of his vision. I leave it to the reader to decide who is guilty of projective distortion in this instance.

[18] Indeed, we might say something similar with regard to the distorting influence of the *animus* in the experience of certain female authors, with regard to their perception of expressions of male sexuality.

[19] In her essay "Reductionism/Finalism and the Child," Chapter 4 of this book, Patricia Berry takes up the issue of fact versus metaphor in the understanding of victimization. Depending upon the therapeutic intent at a particular moment of therapy with a particular individual, one might choose to speak with the patient as though everything reported were fact, for the reason that when speaking to a victim one is often speaking to the figure of a child, and "the child asks for certainty (not ambiguity)." Indeed, Berry suggests, "that, at times, it may be important to imagine things as even more literal than may be the case" (1997, 86). The question of historical truth here takes backseat to therapeutic expediency, which leans toward the "pragmatic truth" of an interpretation (see Spence 1982)

Bibliography

Adler, A. [1910] 1978. *Co-operation between the Sexes: Writings on Women and Men, Love and Marriage, and Sexuality*, edited and translated by H.L. Ansbacher and R.R. Ansbacher. New York: Norton.

Allen, J. and J.M. Young, eds. 1989. *The Thinking Muse: Feminism and Modern French Philosophy*. Bloomington: Indiana University Press.

de Beauvoir, S. [1949] 1989. *The Second Sex*, translated by H.M. Parshley. New York: Vintage Books.

Berry, P. 1997. "Reduction/Finalism and the Child." In *Fire in the Stone: The Alchemy of Soul-making*, edited by Stanton Marlan, 79-93. Wilmette, Illinois: Chiron.

Bruehl-Young, E., ed. 1990. *Freud on Women: A Reader*. New York: Norton.

Butler, J. [1981] 1989. "Sexual Ideology and Phenomenological Description: A Feminist Critique of Merleau-Ponty's *Phenomenology of Perception*." In *The Thinking Muse: Feminism and Modern French Philosophy*, edited by J. Allen and I.M. Young. Bloomington: Indiana University Press.

Chodorow, N. 1978. *The Reproduction of Mothering: Psychoanalysis and the Sociology of Gender*. Berkeley: University of California Press.

———. 1994. *Femininities, Masculinities, Sexualities: Freud and Beyond*. Lexington: University Press of Kentucky.

Churchill, S.D. 1993. "Forbidden Pleasure: Male Desire for (and) Identification with the Female Body." 101st Annual Convention of the American Psychological Association, August, Toronto.

Derrida, J. 1985. *The Ear of the Other*. New York: Schocken.

Dinnerstein, D. 1976. *The Mermaid and the Minotaur: Sexual Arrangements and Human Malaise*. New York: Harper & Row.

Erikson, E. 1968. *Identity: Youth and Crisis*. New York: Norton.

Freud, S. [1937] 1964. "Analysis Terminable and Interminable." In *The Standard Edition of the Complete Psychological Works of Sigmund Freud*, edited and translated by J. Strachey, 23: 209-53. London: The Hogarth Press.

———. [1925] 1990. "Some Psychical Consequences of the Anatomical Distinction between the Sexes." In *Freud on Women: A Reader*, edited by E. Bruehl-Young. New York: Norton.

Herrmann, A. 1991. "'Passing' Women, Performing Men." In *The Female Body: Figures, Styles, Speculations,* edited by L. Goldstein, 178-89. Ann Arbor: University of Michigan Press.

Hillman, J. 1983. *Healing Fiction.* Dallas: Spring Publications.

Jung, C.G. [1935] 1953. "The Relations between the Ego and the Unconscious." In *Two Essays on Analytical Psychology,* edited by Jung and translated by R.F.C. Hull. Princeton: Princeton University Press.

———. [1955/1956] 1970. *Mysterium Coniunctionis: An Inquiry into the Separation and Synthesis of Psychic Opposites in Alchemy,* translated by R.F.C. Hull. Princeton: Princeton University Press.

Kaplan, L. 1991. *Female Perversions: The Temptations of Emma Bovary.* New York: Doubleday.

Merleau-Ponty, M. [1945] 1962. *Phenomenology of Perception,* translated by C. Smith. London: Routledge & Kegan Paul.

———. [1960] 1964. *The Primacy of Perception and Other Essays.* Evanston: Northwestern University Press.

———. [1964] 1968. *The Visible and the Invisible,* translated by A. Lingis. Evanston: Northwestern University Press.

Monick, E. 1991. *Castration and Male Rage.* Toronto: Inner City Books.

Piraldi, J.-A. 1989. "Female Eroticism in the Work of Simone de Beauvoir." In *The Thinking Muse: Feminism and Modern French Philosophy,* edited by J. Allen and I.M. Young. Bloomington: Indiana University Press.

Riviere, J. 1929. "Womanliness as a Masquerade." *International Journal of Psycho-Analysis* 10: 303-13.

Rubin, L. 1983. *Intimate Strangers: Men and Women Together.* New York: Harper & Row.

Sacher-Masoch, W. von. [1907] 1990. *The Confessions of Wanda von Sacher-Masoch,* translated by M. Phillips, C. Hebert, and V. Vale. San Francisco: RE/SEARCH Publications.

Sartre, J.-P. [1939] 1948. *The Emotions: Outline for a Theory,* translated by B. Frechtman. New York: Citadel Press.

——. [1940] 1948. *The Psychology of Imagination*. New York: Citadel Press.

——. [1936] 1957. *The Transcendence of the Ego*, translated by F. Williams and R. Kirkpatrick. New York: Noonday Press.

——. [1943] 1956. *Being and Nothingness: An Essay in Phenomenological Ontology*, translated by H. Barnes. New York: The Philosophical Library.

Shaktini, N. 1989. "Displacing the Phallic Subject." In *The Thinking Muse: Feminism and Modern French Philosophy*, edited by J. Allen and I.M. Young. Bloomington: Indiana University Press.

Spence, D.P. 1982. *Narrative Truth and Historical Truth: Meaning and Interpretation in Psychoanalysis*. New York: Norton.

Stoller, R.J. 1985. *Observing the Erotic Imagination*. New Haven: Yale University Press.